YOU & YOUR PROPERTY in SPAIN

DAVID SEARL

SANTANA BOOKS

You & Your Property in Spain
Published by Ediciones Santana S.L.
Apartado 41,
29650 Mijas Pueblo (Málaga), Spain
Tel: (0034) 952 485 838. Fax: (0034) 952 485 367
info@santanabooks.com
www.santanabooks.com

Design by Chris Fajardo

Printed in Spain by Gráficas San Pancracio S.L.

Depósito Legal: MA-1.224/2005
ISBN: 84-89954-46-1

CONTENTS

1   BUYING A PROPERTY

You're right. You should have bought a holiday home or a retirement residence in Spain two years ago. Depending on the area, you would have seen an average 30 per cent rise in the value of your property, and even more in some areas.

Do not despair. Even though the market has slowed today, experts predict that prices of Spanish property will continue to rise for the immediate future, and that they certainly will not drop. This means that you are still in time to make a sensible purchase that will bring you pleasure and keep your investment safe.

You have a wide choice of sunshine property available to you now. New construction of high quality continues all over Spain and particularly in the Mediterranean areas as well as in the major cities of Madrid and Barcelona. Mortgage rates, at under 4 per cent, are at record lows and not expected to rise soon. Spanish property sellers are also giving prospective purchasers good terms and more professional service.

Nevertheless, the foreign buyer needs to take care. Too many purchasers seem to leave their common sense at the airport when they enter Spain.

You need sound legal advice from a Spanish professional who may be a lawyer, a registered estate agent, a specialised *gestor*, or an *administrador de fincas*, any of whom is qualified to act in your interests and make sure you are protected and well-advised in the transaction.It's foolish to depend entirely on the seller of the property to make sure you are treated fairly.

Let's give the basic "Buyer Beware" warning first. It goes like this: Believe Nothing. Check Everything.

When they say there is no outstanding mortgage, check the Property Registry. When they say it measures 145 square metres, measure it. When they say the terrace is included, check the plans. Any reputable seller will be perfectly happy to have his offers checked.

This section will advise buyers on how to make legal checks of many points in their purchase.

REAL ESTATE AGENTS

Let's start at the beginning. Your first contact when you decide to buy property in Spain will almost certainly be the estate agent.

In many countries, an estate agent is a registered professional who can be held financially responsible if he intermediates in a sale and the terms later turn out to be falsely based.

In Spain there is no law regulating real estate agents. Anyone at all may act as intermediary in property sales. This means it is difficult to hold an estate agent responsible when a purchase goes wrong. Citizens of Scandinavian countries, or the UK, for example, where consumers are more carefully protected, even from their own mistakes, should be warier in Spain.

There are, however, two professional associations which require examinations and set standards for their members. One of these offers the title of *Agente de la Propiedad Inmobiliaria*, or API for short. The other is the GIPE, the *Gestor Intermediario de Propiedades y Edificios*. You will do well to deal with an estate agent who holds one of these titles.

Even so, if your Spanish estate agent causes you to suffer loss, either through negligence or honest error, you will have a hard time obtaining any recompense. Ask your agent if he carries Professional Indemnity Insurance, and, if so, how much. You may again be surprised to find that most estate agents have either no insurance at all or a minimum amount required by the official Spanish agent's association. Ask your agent if he operates a Bonded Client's Account, into which any deposits will be placed, and which is untouchable except for the stated purpose of the deposit. Here is what can happen if you pay your deposit directly to the seller.

A British couple found a villa they liked on the Costa del Sol. They agreed a price of 180,000, and they transferred a deposit of 18,000, 10 per cent of the price, to reserve the villa from its German owners.

The British couple used a Spanish lawyer plus the advice of a British property agent working in Spain and they felt all was well. The couple sold their home in the UK, shipped their furniture to Spain, wound up their business, and came to Spain for the closing of the sale, when they would pay the rest of the price and sign the deed.

Just before the date with the Notary, their lawyer received a message from the German sellers, saying they could not make it that day and that they would be in touch later. This set off alarm bells with everybody involved. It turned out that the owners had in fact sold the property a month earlier for 210,000 to another buyer, had kept the 18,000 deposited with them, and had left Spain for parts unknown.

Of course the unfortunate British buyers have a clear case against the German sellers for breach of contract, with the right to recover their deposit, plus damages and loss, but how are they going to find them? In fact, they have the right to a sum twice the amount of the deposit if the seller backs out of the deal.

In many European countries, the buyers would also have a case against the estate agent and perhaps the lawyer as well for negligence in performing their services. In Spain they also have a case but where standards are less strict and where the lawyer and estate agent declare that they simply followed accepted practice and were just as dismayed as their clients, a Spanish court might well accept their arguments.

So, be sure to take care that any deposit you make goes into that escrow account, a blocked account, where neither party can get at it until the sale is closed.

In a few cases, unscrupulous estate agents have taken advantage of distressed or innocent sellers, telling them that they can obtain only a very low price for their property. This might be a widow, who has returned to her home country and wants to sell her Spanish property because she needs the money. The agent tells her he can get only 90,000 for the property.

She had the idea it must be worth 120,000 or more in today's brisk market, but she lets herself be convinced. The agent also convinces her to sign an agreement which authorises him to keep anything he can get over that price. The agent then sells the property for 125,000, just as he knew he could, making himself a "commission" of 35,000.

The buyer makes out the cheque to the estate agent, who puts 35,000 in his own account and 90,000 to the owner. All legal and in order. He never tells the seller what he sold it for, and since the buyer and seller never come into contact, the truth is never discovered. Even if it was, the agent has done nothing illegal. After all, the seller signed the agreement, didn't she? This sort of sharp operating becomes a great temptation for agents where owners are often absentee and ignorant.

Even the final figure of the purchase price on the sales contract may be the under-declared amount of 90,000. Since the agent is acting with a power of attorney to sign the contract for the absentee seller, nothing could be done about it after the fact, in any case.

These cases and others like them make a powerful argument for using a Spanish lawyer when you buy property. I will say it again and again. You should use a Spanish lawyer when you buy property in Spain. You should use a lawyer in your own country when you buy property. Why should it be different in Spain?

Having stated this warning, we find that most Spanish estate agents, or foreigners selling property in Spain, are both registered and honest. They only want to make a fair commission by selling good properties which will make their buyers and sellers both happy. Be careful anyway.

COMMISSIONS IN COASTAL AREAS

Most Europeans will be surprised to find that estate agents dealing with Spanish holiday property take commissions starting at five per cent and going up to 10 per cent. These high commissions, say the agents, are justified because they have to deal with many unusual factors in a market where a buyer comes from one country and the seller from another and the transaction takes place in Spain, a third country. They also cite high marketing expenses from international advertising.

Let's just say that, when you are in the final stages of negotiating your purchase price, even the amount of the estate agent's commission might come on the table for a little reduction. Keep in mind that the API, for example, recommends three per cent commission for its agents in most areas of Spain.

Spain has all sorts of estate agents, ranging from the small office in the High Street, who has been in the town for many years and knows everybody personally, to the most modern international real estate offices, filled with computers. Some of the major agencies can contact their offices in Frankfurt or London by Internet, and screen you five views of their offerings right there on the computer. In addition, there are many "Euro agents" of all nationalities who quite legally operate in Spain, although their credentials may not be as well established.

One of these agents should be able to find the property you are looking for. Very few agents in Spain are exclusive, so you might even find two agents showing you the same property.

The estate agent is working for the seller, so his presentation of the property will be the most favourable one, and you should check the facts carefully through your own representative. A reputable estate agent will be very happy to have you verify any of his information through your own lawyer, for example.

YOUR SPANISH LAWYER

Quite a number of Spanish lawyers who practise in areas where foreigners settle speak excellent English or other languages and are accustomed to dealing with foreign residents in Spain.

How to find a good Spanish lawyer? Good question. Here is perhaps the only area in which you can ask advice from people you know. Ask around until you find some satisfied clients.

This is perhaps the only situation in which you can get the right advice by walking into a bar and asking the people if anyone knows a good lawyer. Everybody in the place will have a story about either a good lawyer or a bad one.

Consulates also maintain lists of lawyers who speak the language of their nationality, English, German, and so on. These lists do not mean that the lawyers are the most highly regarded.

How much will it cost? Figure the lawyer to charge you around one per cent of the value of the transaction, unless there are some unusual complications. Settle this with him before you start.

WHAT TO WATCH OUT FOR

Both the European Union and the Spanish government have investigated fraud reports in holiday property, revealing the presence of illegal urbanisations where unwary buyers end up having problems of unpaid taxes, unregistered title deeds, and difficulty in obtaining municipal services or building permission. Spaniards have also been defrauded and problems with house purchase make up a principal area of complaint for the Spanish consumer associations.

To make sure your urbanisation is legal and registered, ask to see the *plan parcial* approved by your *Ayuntamiento,* or town hall. The *plan parcial* is not a partial plan, as it sounds, but the plan of *parcelas,* or building plots, which must be approved. This assures you that your urbanisation is legal. If the developer cannot show you the approved *plan parcial,* you may have problems later with municipal services such as light and water, with your community of property owners and even to obtain from the developer all the elements promised in the sale.

If it is on the beach, make sure that the development is approved by the *Jefatura de Costas* as well as the town hall. Spain's 1988 *Ley de Costas,* the Law of Coasts, empowers the authorities to restrict building and control height and density within 100 metres of the high-water mark.

NEW PROPERTIES

In the case of a new property, you want to make sure that the property has been declared to Hacienda for IBI, as you can incur more fines for not registering it. Make sure that your developer has made a *declaración de obra nueva,* a declaration of new building, and has paid the small tax associated with this, as well. Make sure that your *escritura* mentions the house you have purchased as well as the plot of land on which it stands. Sometimes the deed only refers to the land.

This makes you the owner of anything standing on the land, of course, but you may find yourself subject to taxes and fines relating to an undeclared building. Even worse, you may have bought an illegally constructed house which can never be registered because of zoning regulations. Check this at your town hall *Urbanismo* department.

Sometimes, the purchase of an undeclared building can even work in your favour, but you will need expert advice to make sure you stay within the law. Once you are sure that the building can in fact be registered, you make a contract to purchase only the land from the seller. That's all he has title to, anyway. The price for the land alone is much lower than the price for the land and house together, for a considerable saving on the property transfer tax. This tax is 6 per cent in most areas but 7 per cent in Andalusia. You purchase the house separately by a private contract.

Then the new buyer makes the *declaración de obra nueva*, just as if he himself has built the house. Building permits and other papers are necessary for this, but it can all be arranged, and the buyer will pay only one half of one per cent, compared to the transfer tax of 6 or 7 per cent. It has been done but sound legal advice should be taken because the plan will not work in all areas and situations.

BUYING OFF PLAN

If you are in no hurry to occupy your sunshine property, or if you are buying as an investment to maximise your returns, the "off-plan" purchase offers big savings.

Buying off-plan means that you start paying for your property before construction has even started, with only the plans to look at. The typical construction process runs about 18 months. By the time you have finished your payments, as the builder finishes your flat, you will be looking at a capital increase of 20 per cent or more, sometimes much more. As an investment, it certainly looks better than the stagnant value of stocks and shares today.

However, a thousand things can go wrong with the construction process. Keep in mind that many projects are delivered late, sometimes many months late. Builders are often tempted to cut corners on the quality, figuring that the buyers will accept a lower quality for some items rather than go to court for a lengthy battle for their rights. You want to make sure in your contract that your early stage payments do not go directly to the developer, but into an escrow account to which the developer has no access until the flat is finished and delivered to you. Most of today's respectable developers offer this plan. The bank guarantees the sums you have paid if anything goes wrong. Even so, getting your money back is a poor second best. You want the property, now worth 20 per cent more than you paid for it.

This system has a small extra cost but it means that you are safe if the builder has problems. It also avoids the chance of outright fraud, where a developer simply takes the money and disappears.

This sort of fraud was frequent in the 1980s and is rarely seen today but it does happen. In Seville, for example, 67 Spanish families put down deposits on villas in a new urbanisation outside the city, only to discover that the promoters had not even bought the land, let alone begun building the villas. They are suing to recover their money but the back-logged Spanish courts are moving very slowly.

TOWN URBAN PLAN

It is also important to have a look at the town planning maps of the area around you. A newly prosperous Spain is improving the road system all around the country. What if one of those highways is planned for the bottom of your garden? You can find out from the town's urban plan. This plan is called the *Plan General de Ordenación Urbana*, the PGOU for short. If you yourself cannot read plans, and few of us can, have your lawyer do it.

BEFORE YOU SIGN ANYTHING

Before you sign anything in Spain, even a small reservation deposit agreement, there are some pieces of paper you should see. These include:

1. The seller's own title, known as the *escritura pública*, and a report from the Property Registry called a *nota simple*. In the case of off-plan, you want to see the developer's building permit and plans.

2. The paid-up receipt for his annual property tax, the IBI.

3. The Catastral Certificate giving the exact boundaries and square metres of area.

4. Paid-up receipts for the annual fees of the Community of Property Owners, the Statutes of the Community, and the minutes of the last AGM.

1. *ESCRITURA PÚBLICA*

The *Escritura Pública* is the registered title deed of the property. It is inscribed in the *Registro de la Propiedad*, the Property Registry, and it is the only ironclad guarantee of title in Spain. If your seller cannot produce an *escritura pública*, something is wrong. In this title deed you will find a description of the property, the details of the owner. If any mortgages or court embargoes exist against the property, they will be registered here as marginal notes. You want to see the seller's title deed, if only to make sure that he really is the owner of the property being sold to you.

Your lawyer can obtain a *nota simple* from the Registry, containing the pertinent details and notes of any mortgages against the property. As of 2002, you can obtain a *nota simple* very rapidly on the Internet if you are entered in the Registry program. However, it would be best if you could see a copy of the complete deed.

Strange things can happen with deeds. In one recent case, a widow was selling her property in Spain. However, living in another country, it had never occurred to her to declare the death of her husband in Spain, and his name was still entered on the title deed as half owner of the property. This was done in perfect innocence, because she simply considered herself the full owner of the property when her husband died.

By Spanish law a property held jointly in two names cannot be sold without the signatures of both parties. Because no one had seen the full *escritura* before the scheduled closing and final payment, the fact did not come to light until both parties were ready to sign at the Spanish Notary. The signing had to be postponed for months until the widow could declare her husband's death, which had happened 10 years before, prove that she was the heir, formally accept the inheritance, re-register the property in her own name, and finally sign to sell it. One fortunate consequence of her error was that she did not have to pay any Spanish inheritance tax, because the demand for the tax lapses after five years. Some people do this deliberately, but her lack of action was inadvertent.

All this inheritance settlement could have taken place early in the negotiations if the title deed had been available for examination. You will do well to insist on seeing the complete *escritura*. It's a good idea to know that the seller is really the owner of the property, after all.

2. CHECK IBI RECEIPT

One very important paper you must see before purchasing any second-hand Spanish property is the *Impuesto sobre Bienes Inmuebles* (IBI), the municipal real estate tax. When purchasing from the second or third owner, you must always ask to see the latest paid-up receipt for the IBI before you sign any contract with the seller. If he doesn't have it, you may find yourself liable for back taxes and penalties. Here again your lawyer or property consultant will have valuable advice. A new property bought from a developer will not have an IBI receipt yet and it will be your responsibility to register the property for this tax.

The IBI receipt will show the property's catastral reference number and also your *valor catastral*, the official assessed value of the property. This is a very important figure because various taxes are based on it. (See section on Taxes). The assessed value is almost always considerably less than the real market value, but it has been steadily raised over the last few years.

Your annual real estate tax is charged by the municipality, It can be as low as 120 if you own a small cottage in one of the typical villages, or as much as 2,000 a year if you own a new luxury villa on acres of land near Marbella.

A surcharge of 20 per cent will be placed on the bill if it is not paid on time. You can arrange to have this bill paid directly through your bank, in order to avoid forgetting it. You fill out the forms authorising the bank to pay it, and the tax people will send the bill directly to the bank. In many municipalities those who pay their IBI tax early get discounts of 10 per cent, and a standing order at the bank will ensure that this is done.

So when buying an older property, whether apartment or villa, you want to see the last IBI receipt. If not available, something is amiss. Really, you want to see the IBI receipts for the last five years, not just the current one, because you can be liable for five years of back tax.

The current IBI receipt must be presented to the Notary at the signing of the contract, because it contains the catastral reference number, but you as the buyer want to see it well before that.

3. *REFERENCIA CATASTRAL*

Every property sale must include a mention of the *Referencia Catastral*. As noted above, this reference number appears on your IBI receipt.

The *Catastro* is a second system of property registration, concentrating on the exact location, physical description and boundaries of property, unlike the Property Registry, which focuses on ownership and title. The *Catastro* is also concerned with the valuation of property and is the source of the famous *valor catastral*, the assessed value of property for tax purposes.

These two systems, strangely enough, have never even communicated with each other, and we find that the catastral description of a property sometimes differs greatly from the one in the Property Registry.

As a first step in trying to bring the physical reality into line with statements people sometimes make in contracts, the Spanish authorities have begun to require that all property transactions now include at least a mention of the Catastro reference number in addition to the *escritura*.

It is a very good idea for the buyer to request the actual certification from the Catastro with a full description of the property. If it matches the data given in your contract, you are all right. If there are large differences, perhaps something is wrong.

The certification itself comes in two parts, one being a description in words of the property and the other being a graphic representation, either a plan or an aerial photo. Get both of them. It costs only a few euros, although it can take up to two months for the Catastro to deliver the certificates, so you had better start early.

It is astonishing how often the boundaries and square metres of a property can differ so much. This is because people through the years have simply accepted the vague descriptions made in the title deed, and do not check any further. Be warned that, when you ask the seller or the estate agent for this catastral certificate, they will pooh-pooh the idea, saying it is not legally necessary yet, although it will be in the future. Do not pay much attention to them. Insist on getting it, so you can be sure of your real boundaries and the real size of the property.

The Notary is also empowered to call attention to the fact that discrepancies exist between the Catastro and Property Registry descriptions. The buyer and seller can go ahead with their transaction, but they have been advised of the discrepancy.

4. COMMUNITY FEES, STATUTES AND MINUTES OF AGM

If you are buying a flat, a townhouse, or a villa on an urbanisation, ask also to see the latest paid-up receipt for community fees. These are the fees charged by your *Comunidad de Propietarios,* the Community of Property Owners, which is the Spanish term for "condominium", meaning the legal body that controls all the elements held in common. In a building this would be the lift, gardens and pool for example.

In an urbanisation, the Community as a whole jointly owns the roads, gardens, pool, lighting system and other elements as well. Each owner is assigned a quota, or percentage of the expenses, which he must pay, by law. See the section on Communities for full details. Just remember that you become a member of the Community, with legal rights and obligations, just by purchasing your property. Only those who buy a country property or a house on a normal street in a town will not have to deal with Community problems.

The receipt for Community fees assures you that the fees are paid and gives you a good idea of your monthly charges in the future.

Read the Statutes, the regulations, of the community, too, as they will be binding on you once you have signed the purchase contract. If the basic Statutes that rule the Community prohibit the keeping of pets in the building or on the estate, you will have real problems if you want to keep your dogs, for example. Get a copy of these Statutes in a language you can read, even if the Spanish regulations are the only valid ones.

Then you want to see the Minutes Book, the official record, of the last Annual General Meeting of the Community. Decisions are taken by majority vote of the owners at each year's AGM, and these actions are recorded in the Minutes Book, which is an official document. If you find that the principal point at last year's meeting was how to solve the Community's chronic water shortage, then you will know you are going to have problems in your new house. Talk to the President of the Community if this is possible. A well-run Community can add thousands of euros to a property's value, and a Community with problems is a source of endless aggravation.

UTILITIES BILLS

You want to see paid-up receipts for the owner's electricity, water, rubbish collection, and even telephone. This assures you that the bills are paid and also gives you an idea of what it will cost to run the place.

If you wind up stuck with unpaid bills by the previous owner, be aware that these are personal bills from private companies. They do not attach to the property, only to the person who signed the electric or water company contract. The company will insist that they will cut off the service if the bills are not paid. Let them cut it off. For a reasonable fee, you simply go into the company office and sign a new contract, starting fresh without the previous owner's bills. This fee is exactly the same as the charge for changing the electricity contract into your own name in any case.

Once you and your lawyer or adviser are satisfied with these checks into the situation of the property, and you and the seller have arrived at a price, you can factor into your calculations the amount of taxes and fees that will be paid on the transaction.

TRANSFER COSTS

What are the taxes and fees going to cost you? They will probably be less than 10 per cent of the purchase price if the breaks are with you, but can go as high as 15 per cent if certain taxes turn out to be higher than usual in your individual case.

You have two taxes and two fees to pay on the transfer of property. The two fees are for the notarisation of the deed and for its registry in the Property Registry. The two taxes are the transfer tax and a sort of capital gains tax on the increase in value of the land, usually called the *plus valia* tax. This last tax is a municipal tax.

Notary: You pay the *Notario* a fee fixed by an official scale. The fee varies according to the amount of land, the size of the dwelling and its price, but let's say between   350 and   600.

Property Registry: Then there is a fee for the inscription of the property in your name in the official *Registro de la Propiedad.* This will be somewhat less. Your lawyer or property consultant can tell you exactly how much these fees will be before you buy.

Transfer Tax: The transfer tax, called *Impuesto de Transmisiones Patrimoniales* in Spanish, is 6 per cent of the value declared in the contract for private sales. If you purchase new property from a developer, this tax will be IVA (value added tax), at 7 per cent because the sale is a business operation, not a private deal between two individuals. In addition to this, you pay a documents fee, or stamp duty, of one half of one per cent, so buying a new property will draw tax of 7.5 per cent.

In Andalusia, the transfer tax has been raised to 7 per cent and the stamp duty raised to one full percent, making the total charge 8 per cent in both cases.

Plus Valia: The other tax on property sales is the *arbitrio sobre el incremento del valor de los terrenos,* the municipal tax on the increase in the value of the land since its last sale. This is usually called the *plus valia* for short, and it can vary widely. In the case of an apartment or a townhouse in a new urbanisation, where little land is involved and where there has been no real increase in value because such a short time has passed since it was developed, the tax can be very low. It will be much higher if you buy a house with several thousand square metres of land, which has not changed hands for 20 years and which has been recently re-zoned from rural to urban land, thus jumping greatly in value.

This tax is based on the official value of the land, which is always lower than the market value, and it varies from 10 per cent up to 40 per cent of the annual increase, depending on the length of time between sales and the town where it is located. The land is officially re-valued periodically for this purpose.

Do not confuse this *plus valía* tax with the non-resident's 35 per cent capital gains tax on profits from the sale. (See Tax section).

You can find out exactly how much your *plus valía* will be simply by going into the municipal tax office in your town and asking. They keep the records there for each property and will be glad to tell you the assessed value, so you can find out in advance. Or have your lawyer or property consultant do it.

The *plus valía* tax is charged directly to the property itself. If an unscrupulous seller promises to pay it but somehow forgets, the new owner is stuck with paying it, or losing the property, so make sure it is paid.

WHO PAYS WHAT?

The buyer and seller are free to contract whatever terms they choose. There is no Spanish law which requires that one of the parties must pay any particular tax.

Traditionally, the seller has paid the notary's fees and the *plus valía* tax, as he is the one making the profit on the increase in the land's value. The buyer pays the *impuesto de transmisiones* and the registry fee, as he is the one who is interested in making sure the property is truly registered in his name. Spanish consumer regulations state that this should be the normal division of costs.

It is a frequent practice, however, for the contract to state that the buyer will pay *todos los gastos,* all the expenses arising. There is nothing illegal about this. Remember that the two parties are free to make any contract they choose.

This practice, which may seem unfair to the buyer, has come about because tax bills, especially the *plus valía,* have often gone unpaid, especially by non-resident sellers. By the time the new purchaser realised this, the seller was gone and the buyer stuck with the taxes anyway, as they were billed to the owner of the property if the seller did not pay.

Charging the new owner with all the taxes is at least straightforward and avoids complications.

Nevertheless, you can use this point in negotiating your final price. If the contract you are offered states that you as the purchaser must pay all taxes and fees, you could suggest that the seller take something off the price.

Finally, you have your lawyer's fee, or the fee to the *administrador de fincas* or *gestor* who has advised you. A lawyer's fee may be as little as 500 if he has merely vetted your contract, found it good, handled the basic paperwork and encountered no complications. It can be much higher if the *abogado* has to sort out complications.

As a rough guide, figure one per cent of the price as a standard lawyer's fee. Some lawyers charge less, many try to charge more.

HOW MUCH TO DECLARE?

Formerly it was the practice to declare a ridiculously low amount for the value of the house, in order to minimise the transfer tax, but now Spanish lawyers advise sellers and buyers to declare the approximate market value, normally the real value of the sale. Spanish tax inspectors will make their own assessment if they feel the declaration is too low.

The Hacienda ministry, Spain's tax agency, maintains its own tables of values on property, and they are empowered to set a higher value on a sale if they judge the declaration to be under market value. More than one property purchaser has been disconcerted to discover that he has to pay extra taxes when he gets a new tax bill six months after the sale.

If they discover that the transfer has been under-declared by more than 12,000 and 20 per cent, they can apply heavy penalties to both the buyer and seller under the terms of Spain's 1989 *Ley de Tasas* — the law of public fees — which was enacted to prevent precisely this dodge.

In doubt, you can ask the tax office what value they will accept on any particular property. Inquire at the *oficina liquidadora*, the payment office, at your nearest tax agency office, and they will tell you exactly what value they assign to your purchase. They base their valuation on a careful study of various factors, such as location, size, quality, age, and others. Or just do as more and more people are doing today, and declare the actual amount of the sale.

Buyer Beware: When you go to resell your property, you will be charged Spanish capital gains tax on any profit you make. If you are a resident, you pay as part of your income tax with a maximum of 15 per cent. If you are non-resident, you face the 35 per cent capital gains tax on the profits you have made. If you declare a low value now, you will be liable for tax on a much bigger profit when you sell later. It is in your own best interests, as the buyer, to declare the full amount of the sale. (See section on taxes for more details.)

THE CONTRACT

Let's suppose that you have found a property that suits you, that all of the pre-purchase checks have satisfied you, and you have negotiated the price down to what you can pay. Keep in mind that very few sellers will not come down on the price. Make an offer and see what happens.

Terms of the sales contract will be your next concern.

Because most buyers take some time to assemble the cash needed for the purchase, it is usual for the buyer and seller to make a "private contract " first, with the buyer putting down a non-returnable deposit of, say 10 per cent. This reserves the property while the buyer brings his money into Spain or perhaps obtains a Spanish mortgage. If the buyer fails to complete the sale, he loses the amount of his deposit.

If the seller finds another buyer in the meantime, willing to pay more, and sells the property, the first buyer can claim twice the amount of the deposit back.

Remember never to pay the deposit directly to the seller. Make sure that it goes into an escrow account, a blocked account, called a Bonded Client Account, from which it will not be released until the sale is final. Insist on this.

The seller, through the estate agent, will certainly have a prepared private contract all ready for you to sign. The contract they offer may suit you perfectly, but it is quite likely that it will contain some clauses more favourable to the seller than to you, the buyer. This is when you want your lawyer to read the contract and make suggestions.

It is a very good idea to have the contract made in Spanish, with a translation into English or German or your native language, so you can be absolutely sure about what you are signing.

Although most property sales between individuals follow this system of private contract and deposit, followed by closing and final payment, there is nothing binding about it. If you like the property and have the price ready, you can proceed directly to the Notary, pay over the full price, and get your title deed.

This private contract, although it sets out all the details of the agreement, such as payment terms and who pays what share of the taxes, is not the final document for the sale.

ESCRITURA DE COMPRAVENTA

This final document is the *escritura de compraventa* and it must be signed by you and the seller in the presence of a Spanish *Notario* in order to make it legally binding. You can make a *poder* — a power of attorney — allowing another person to sign for you if you cannot be present. (See section below for more on Power of Attorney). The *Notario,* or Notary, is an official of the State who makes sure that contracts are legal. He keeps the original document in his files in case any question arises later. The *Notario* is a public official, not a private lawyer. His duty is to certify that the contract has been signed, the money paid, and that the purchaser and seller have been advised of their tax obligations.

He does not verify or guarantee the accuracy of the statements made in the contract. He only certifies that the parties have signed it properly. Too many people think that the *Notario* assures them that all statements made in the contract are true. This is not so. The Notary can, however, give useful advice to both parties.

POWER OF ATTORNEY

A "General Power of Attorney" a *poder general,* is frequently used in Spain. The power comes in a standard form, which lists all of the actions that can be carried out by the holder. These include buying and selling property, handling bank accounts, spending and receiving money, taking out a mortgage or other loan, and just about anything that the person himself can do with his assets.

The form contains a clause declaring that all of these actions shall be taken for the benefit of the granter of the power. This means that, if you decide to take the money and run, the granter has a case against you for defrauding him, if he can find you.

There are also other forms of power of attorney, limited to carrying out certain specific actions in the name of the granter, such as signing a contract for the sale of a specified property at a given price, during a given time period, after which the power lapses.

But the general power is the one most used, simply because situations change and unforeseen complexities arise in any transaction.

This can mean that the holder of the power is unable to act because the power does not mention the specific circumstance which has arisen, such as signing at the bank to obtain the money transfer from abroad.

The wide powers of the general power of attorney avoid these problems. In an international property market, we often find that a seller or a buyer cannot be physically present at the moment of signing a purchase deed at the Spanish Notary, so he gives his lawyer or some other trusted person a general power of attorney to sign for him.

Once the deed is accomplished, the granter then revokes the power of attorney, again at the Notary, and all goes on as before.

You make the *poder general* at the Spanish Notary. Although it is always a good idea to consult a lawyer before taking any important legal step, it is not necessary. The Notary has the power of attorney forms, probably in his computer, which will print copies for you while the Notary himself retains the original power of attorney. A reminder: you need copies authorised by the Notary in order to use the power of attorney at a bank or in a property sale. The simple copies you can also obtain are for information only.

The only documents necessary are the national identity document or the passport of the maker of the power. He will need the name and identity document or passport details of the holder. The entire operation should not cost much more than   60.

The recipient of the power of attorney does not need to appear at the Notary. The document requires his signature, but he can do this at his own convenience. So the maker of the power can simply post it to the recipient.

Contracts can be quite simple or very complicated. If you are paying one lump sum and the property is to be delivered at once, there remains only the question of who is to pay the taxes and fees.

If you are paying over time, there will be a number of further provisions in your contract, relating to the timing and amount of the payments.

The seller might insist on a clause stating that the buyer loses all sums paid out if he fails to keep up the payments, as well as having to vacate the property immediately. In fact, this is always negotiable. If a buyer who cannot keep up the payments takes his case to court, he will find that the court will almost certainly allow him to receive some of his money back in exchange for vacating the property, which he loses.

What he gets back depends on how many payments the buyer has already made, for example. If he has already paid more than half of the full price, the court will not allow the seller to keep it all.

The buyer really needs a Spanish lawyer to make sure this sort of complicated contract is fair to him.

FREE OF CHARGES AND LIENS

One extremely important item in your contract is the clause stating the property is sold free of all charges, liens and mortgages. Fine, you say, but how do you really know this is true?

This is where your lawyer comes in. He can make a check at the property registry, the *Registro de la Propiedad*, where any such mortgages or liens must be registered against the *escritura*. The *Registro de la Propiedad* is an extremely important office for the property purchaser.

Any mortgage on the property must be registered there, and the true owner of the property is listed. For a small fee, the *registro* will give you a *nota simple* for any property. This is a summary of the property's entry into the registry books, which would include a reference to any mortgages pending on the property.

Such a check-up can avoid problems. One horrible case occurred when a British owner returned to Spain to find that his new house had been seized by court order and auctioned off to pay an outstanding mortgage left by the seller. The locks had been changed and the house, for which he had paid, was no longer his.

His only remedy was to sue the fraudulent seller for breach of contract and fraud. That is, if he could find him.

He could also have solved the problem if he had been aware that his property was under threat. If he himself had been present in Spain to receive legal notice of the coming seizure and auction, he could have arranged with the court to pay the mortgage, which attaches to the property itself, not to the previous owner.

Paying the mortgage would have been an unpleasant experience but much cheaper than losing the entire property.

Notices of such legal actions appear by law in the *Boletin Oficial,* the official legal gazette, and often in the local newspapers as well. If the new owner cannot be located by the court, these published notices constitute sufficient legal notice to make the seizure of the property correct in law. Overworked Spanish courts have been severely criticised for failure to make sufficient attempt to locate the absentee owners, but the practice continues.

Your lawyer will also check to make sure that no back taxes are owed on the property and that its original registration is in order. Back taxes must be checked with Hacienda or the town hall. They are just about the only debts not listed at the Property Registry.

CONTRACT MUST DESCRIBE PROPERTY ACCURATELY

The contract must accurately describe the property being sold. This is one area where the catastral certificate is important. Too many buyers have discovered too late that their boundaries are not what they thought, and the hedgerow at the bottom of their garden, an obvious division, is not the legal line at all, but belongs to their neighbour. This sort of error does not necessarily imply bad faith on the part of the seller. He may have happily accepted the boundaries and square metres set out in his title deed, and never checked them.

Remember that we mentioned the *Registro de la Propiedad* is concerned mainly with ownership of property, while the *Catastro* is concerned mainly with the physical measurements and characteristics. The Property Registry is quite often wrong, so get the catastral certificate and be sure.

If you really have problems with boundaries, you should have an official surveyor, a *topógrafo*, come and survey the plot. On a transaction of 200,000, the 500 or so that he charges is very little.

Even those buying apartments will do well to measure their square metres of enclosed space and terraces, to make sure they match the description offered. It is astonishing how often the flat actually has fewer square metres than stated. If you discover this, it may make a bargaining point for getting the price down.

Buyers of rural land will certainly need a property surveyor to measure the land and identify its boundaries. In these cases, even the Catastral department may not have the correct data. The titles to many rural properties state only that the *finca* borders on the north with Juan Garcia's farm, and that is simply not good enough.

CONTRACT MUST IDENTIFY BUYER AND SELLER

The contract must also fully identify the seller and buyer.

Remember that the seller is the owner of the property, not the estate

27

agent handling the deal. It is always a bad practice to make your cheque out to an agency. You should know exactly who the seller is and make your cheque directly to him. If the seller insists on anonymity, meaning a bearer cheque, make sure that no money changes hands until you are actually at the Spanish Notary, where you will sign the final contract.

Make your cheques out only to the name of the seller. In the case of reserve deposits before the sale is completed, and where you may never have met the absentee seller, insist that your cheque be deposited in an escrow account, a Bonded Client Account. Then the money can be paid out only to the seller and only when the specified time limit has elapsed.

FINAL TITLE AND REGISTRATION

In fact, even the *escritura de compraventa* contract does not fully assure your title until it is registered with the Spanish Property Registry, thus making it an *escritura pública*, a public document. It is, in fact, the same document, now registered and with the stamps of the *Registro de la Propiedad* on it.

Notice of the contract signed can be sent by fax directly from the Notary's office, at the time of signing, to the *Registro de la Propiedad*. This notification will ensure that no one else can register the property, until the full contract is presented at the Registry. Or you can have someone deliver the signed contract directly to the Registry. Normally, this will be someone from the Notary's office.

You yourself will never have the original of your *escritura pública*. The original document is stamped at the Property Registry, which converts it from a sales contract into a public document. The document is then returned to the Notary, where it is kept safely on file. If you, or any official body, needs a copy of it, you request it from the Notary, who produces an authorised copy. The copy is what you take home.

In fact, you no longer sign the contract itself. In these modern times of easy and foolproof copying, the parties to the contract sign a blank sheet of paper, and the Notary keeps these samples in his files for later authentication when necessary. So, nobody can copy your signature from a copy of your title deed because it isn't there.

In cases where the same piece of property has been fraudulently sold two or three times, the purchaser who first has it registered will be the owner, regardless of the dates of the other sales.

Slow as the administrative bureaucracy may be, your deed should be registered within a few months. Usually your lawyer or whoever is handling the matter will ask you for a deposit of money in advance to cover the estimated taxes and fees, and will either bill you for the remainder or refund to you the overpayment when the deed is registered. This is normal and acceptable practice.

If the matter seems to drag on for months, you had better look into what is happening. There was a case a few years ago where one property consultant took people's money, put the cash into his own bank account and the *compraventa* deed into a drawer. He used his clients' money for a year or so, enabling him to make down payments on Costa del Sol property, and then, at last, presented the deeds for registry. The registry came through in due course and he notified his clients, who often got a small refund, which made them happy. Everyone assumed that it took a year and a half for the registry to process the papers. This is simply not true.

The reason for haste in delivering the sales contract to the Property Registry is simple. As long as the property continues to be registered in the name of the seller, he can use it to take out a mortgage, for example. The bank checks the Registry, finds the property correctly listed, and grants the seller a mortgage of, say, 120,000 on the villa valued at 180,000. Our criminally-minded seller has prepared this operation well in advance with the innocent bank, but he does not execute it until after the sale has taken place, in the time interval between signing the *compraventa* contract and your registration of it as an *escritura pública*.

Otherwise, you see, you would have found the mortgage listed against the property in the Property Registry when you got your *nota simple*. This is also why it is a good idea to get your *nota simple* immediately before you sign the contract.

The seller then disappears to some other country with the 120,000.

You yourself are perfectly happy with your new property. You are convinced that your pre-purchase checks assured you that the title had no charges against it, which was true at the time.

That is, you are happy for a few years, when you suddenly discover that your property has been sold at a court auction — *subasta* — without your having been informed, and the police are coming with a court order to put you in the street.

How can this be? The bank which is foreclosing the unpaid mortgage of 120,000 and repossessing the property, will inform only the registered owner, which at the time of making the mortgage was the person who sold it to you. The court has no reason to inform you because you do not exist as far as they are concerned. They are repossessing the house of the person who failed to pay the mortgage. These cases have happened.

Or you might find out about the mortgage because the bank in fact checks at the house and finds you there instead of the mortgage-holder.

You protest that you have nothing to do with this situation but, legally, you have no case. The bank acted in good faith and their mortgage claim has preference. Your only choice is whether to pay 120,000 more or to abandon the property. You can then, of course, bring suit against the seller to recover your money. If you can find him.

Such cases are rare, but they happen.

METHOD OF PAYMENT

Give some thought to your method of payment. One point to consider is whether you are buying from a resident or a non-resident.

In the old days before the European Union, property buyers had to pay Spaniards or residents in pesetas, and had to prove importation of foreign currency if they later wanted to export the money from Spain. With the lifting of exchange controls, this is no longer necessary, although a report must be made to the bank.

You can pay for your Spanish property in euros, through a bank cheque, from your Spanish bank, along with a bank certificate that you have imported foreign currency for this purpose. You can also pay by cheque in foreign currency. You can also pay by direct transfer from your foreign bank to the seller's foreign bank, so that no money enters Spain.

CERTIFICATE OF NON-RESIDENCE

If you wish to keep the money transfer completely undocumented inside Spain, you can do this, but you must then obtain a certificate of non-residence from the Spanish authorities. Be warned that this can take up to two months to obtain, and the Notary will not authorise the completion of the sale without it. If you file your bank certificate and use a normal cheque, this certificate is not necessary.

FIVE PER CENT TAX DEPOSIT

If you buy from a non-resident, you must deposit five per cent of the total purchase price with Hacienda in the seller's name, as a guarantee on his taxes. A few sellers, who have owned their Spanish property for a long time, will be exempt from this deposit.

You pay the seller only 95 per cent of the price. You pay the other five per cent directly to Hacienda, presenting Form 211 to justify your payment. The Notary will want to see your copy of Form 211, showing that you have made the payment and filed the form with the Tax Agency.

This amount serves as a guarantee against the non-resident seller's Spanish capital gains tax liability and for his payment of the annual Spanish wealth tax and non-resident property owner's imputed income tax.

Non-resident owners of Spanish property are required to declare two per cent or 1.1 per cent of the official rated value, the *valor catastral,* of their property as if it were income. They then must pay real income tax on this imaginary income. The non-resident pays at a flat rate of 25 per cent. (See section on Taxes for more details).

If Hacienda discovers that the non-resident seller has failed to keep up his yearly imputed income tax payments, they can retain this amount from the deposit of 5 per cent.

The deposit is mainly designed, however, to cover the non-resident's liability for Spain's capital gains tax of 35 per cent on his profit. As of December 31, 1996, Spain ended the exemption from capital gains for those who owned their property more than 10 years. This was replaced by an inflation correction factor that reduces the capital gains tax but can never eliminate it completely, so most non-resident sellers will be liable for some Spanish capital gains tax. (See Tax section for full details on how this works).

PROPERTY PURCHASE CHECK-LIST

1. Advice from a Spanish lawyer or property consultant.

2. The seller's *escritura pública,* or title deed, as registered in the *Registro de la Propiedad.* In the case of new property, the *declaración de obra nueva.* In the case of off-plan, the developer's building permit.

3. A *nota simple* from the Property Registry, showing that no mortgages are registered against the property.

4. *Referencia Catastral.* The number itself appears on the IBI receipt, but you want the full certification document, the *Certificado Catastral,* that describes the property in detail.

5. A check on the legality and *plan parcial* if you buy in an urbanisation, and assurance in writing of a building permit if you buy a plot.

6. A paid-up receipt for the IBI, *Impuesto sobre Bienes Inmuebles,* or the *declaración de obra nueva.*

7. Receipt for paid-up community charges and a copy of the Statutes if you buy in a condominium.

8. Copies of owner's bills for electricity, water, rubbish collection and even the telephone.

9. A contract, in Spanish, and a translation into your own language, with terms you understand.

10. A decision about your form of payment, whether in euros or other currency, and be sure to insist on declaring the full amount.

11. An *escritura de compraventa* signed before a *notario.*

12. Payment of fees and taxes, and the five per cent deposit to Hacienda if you buy from a non-resident, using Form 211.

13. An idea of how and when you will get your final *escritura pública,* which makes you the real owner.

BUYING WITHOUT *ESCRITURA*

Surprisingly often, the seller does not have an *escritura pública,* for perfectly legitimate reasons, or at least for reasons which will not affect you, the purchaser. Perhaps he has not completed his own purchase yet, or it has taken a longer time than usual.

One reason for owning property on a private contract only, without a public title deed, is that the property cannot be seized by the court in order to pay a debt of the owner. Only registered property can be attached by a court. Another reason is simply to avoid the payment of the transfer taxes and fees, which can total 10 per cent or even more of the value. A third reason is, of course, to conceal assets, either from a creditor or the tax man, or an ex-wife, for example. When the Property Register is checked, there is nothing listed under that name.

On the Spanish Costas, where there was a freewheeling property market for some years, many properties changed hands so quickly as buyers sought quick profits that they simply did not register them. They just waited for the next buyer to carry out all the formalities, thus avoiding transfer taxes.

It is possible that a house you fancy has had two or three owners in the last five or six years and that not one of them ever got his final *escritura pública.* It might be that the house does not legally exist, as it has never been declared to the tax authorities in a *declaración de obra nueva.* The only legal document for the property simply refers to the plot of land and does not even mention the house.

Or you might buy a tract of land in the *campo,* the owners of which are seven brothers whose family has owned the land for a hundred years but never had a written document.

There are perfectly legal ways of solving all these problems.

You can have the piece of land made over to you by the original seller, three owners back. You yourself can make the *declaración de obra nueva,* even though you did not build the house.

But be careful. If you want to establish the title through a series of private contracts, you may find that you are liable for quite a lot of back taxes, perhaps two or three *plus valías* which have never been paid by the previous owners. This tax may be charged to the present owner of the property.

205 PROCEDURE

One completely legal and frequently used solution for property which has no registered title at all is called a 205 procedure, after the number of the regulation which controls it. In this process, you obtain from the Property Registry what is called a "negative certification". This means that the Registry has searched its files and finds no registered owner for the property. Here again you will find the *certificado catastral* useful, because it will have an accurate physical description.

You then request that the property be registered in your name because you have bought it from whoever is the seller, who, in turn, justifies his title by whatever document or evidence he presents. This transaction must be published and posted publicly in case anyone wishes to protest. If no protest is made against your claim, at the end of about a year's time you will get a solid title.

If you are going to buy under these conditions, be sure to hold back a percentage of the price until the property is registered in your name. No matter how simple the procedure appears when you start, there is always the possibility of some unknown person coming forward with a claim to the title. There is an element of risk.

EXPEDIENTE DE DOMINIO

This process, roughly translated as an ownership proceeding, requires more time and expense than the 205 procedure, because it involves more investigation and court action. The *expediente de dominio* can also be used to establish title when the property is in fact registered, but in the name of a person who no longer claims it either because he has sold it to someone on a private contract, who has never registered the sale, or perhaps because the original owner has died. This will take about two years.

The claim must be published in the official bulletin and evidence taken in court. Finally, the court will rule on the title and it will be solid. There is always the chance of some nephew who should have inherited the property making a claim of his own against the present purchaser, and the court will decide where the best claim lies.

In any of these procedures to establish title and register the property, be warned that you will be unable to obtain any mortgage funding, and you cannot borrow against the property for two years after its registration.

In any of these cases, you need sound legal advice. Ask around among older residents for an *abogado* or an *administrador de fincas* or a *gestor* whom they trust.

PROPERTY OWNED BY OFFSHORE COMPANY

You might be offered property already owned by an offshore company registered in one of the many "tax havens" around the world.

This means that the property is not registered in the name of the owner. It is registered in the name of a company located in Gibraltar or Panama or the Cayman Islands. The owner of the company owns the property.

These "tax havens" earn their name because they are legal jurisdictions where taxes on locally registered companies are nil or very small, and secrecy is assured from the owner's own tax jurisdiction.

The advantages are clear. When you sell your Spanish property, it is only the company that is transferred. The same company continues to own the same Spanish property, so no Spanish transfer taxes are charged. Only the offshore company has a new owner. The same applies for inheritance tax when the company is bequeathed to an inheritor. The offshore location charges no tax on this.

The disadvantages are that Spain, keenly aware of the tax loss, has placed a flat tax of three per cent per year on any property held by an offshore company. They have a list of tax havens. European Union authorities are also placing restrictions on these companies, so it is becoming a doubtful proposition.

As a buyer, you have a choice between purchasing the off-shore company itself or buying as an individual and paying the transfer taxes.

See section on Taxes for advantages and disadvantages of off-shore companies.

BANK REPOSSESSIONS AND AUCTIONS

After the 1989 crash of the Spanish property boom, the sunshine coasts were littered with real bargains. Some of these bargains were on sale by people who could not keep up the payments on their property, some of them were offered at cut-rate prices by developers who were stuck with stock they couldn't sell, and some of them were villas and apartments that had been repossessed by banks.

Bank foreclosure of mortgages is one of the few Spanish legal procedures that works quickly and effectively. A few of the properties were even those seized by courts and sold at auction to satisfy a debt against the owner, as in several of the frightening examples we have seen earlier in this section.

The standard wisdom today is that all of these bargain properties have been sold, and the few remaining are those which are so undesirable that nobody wants them at any price. This is mainly true, but there are still some bargains available if you look for them.

One of the easiest ways to make a stab at buying a cut-price property is simply to walk into the offices of bank managers in an area where you would like to live. Go into the bank, say that you would like to speak with the manager about a business matter. He will probably speak English and he will probably receive you after a short wait. Tell him you are interested in buying a repossessed property, a *Reposesión*. Ask him if he has any on his books.

You may be as astonished as I was when he points to a stack of *escrituras* on his desk and says, "How about one of these?" If the bank is a bit more modern, he may punch up a list on his computer terminal and inquire about the price range that interests you. So, you look at the list and pick a villa or an apartment that seems promising. You view it, like it, and buy it from the bank for maybe half what it would fetch on the market. It can be that easy. Or you might find that banks in your area do not have anything that interests you.

So why aren't these properties already sold, you ask. Good question. The answer seems to be that banks simply don't know how to sell real estate. A few of them have established their own departments for selling their repossessed properties, but most of them just sit in the files until the court gets around to auctioning them off at official proceedings.

If you really feel like getting into the system, you could even try the court-ordered auctions of property being sold to satisfy debts. These auctions, called *subastas,* can offer some incredible buys to those who get into the inside on how they work. Properties have been sold at one-tenth their real value, for example. Yes, in northern European countries this simply cannot take place, but under the Spanish system the court is obliged to take the highest offer, no matter how low, after the property has been offered several times.

You are right if you think that this system attracts abuses. In many courts, there are professional *subasteros* who work together, sometimes in collusion with corrupt court officials, to offer low bids. Later, these professionals split the take among themselves. They often assign the properties to third parties, who are not real buyers, but who also get their share of the profits once the property is sold on again.

FINANCING BY DEVELOPER

There are a number of ways in which you can finance your Spanish property, just as you probably did when you first purchased a house in your own country. Mortgages of 20 and 30 years, along with mortgages of 100 per cent of the value of the property, are now available in Spain. For a non-resident buyer, however, the mortgage is usually limited to around 70 per cent of the valuation of the property.

Let's look first at financing which may be offered you by the developer of the project where you purchase. There are dozens of different schemes here and you should be wary.

The contract must stipulate the down payment, enumerate the following payments and state when such payments end. It will be clear from the total of these payments just how much the developer's financing will cost you in comparison to paying cash. If the difference is acceptable to you, you have a deal.

Make sure you know what happens if you miss a payment. There should be some provision which is not too harmful to you, allowing you to make a certain number of late payments for only a small penalty.

Another essential provision will allow you to pay off the remainder of the contract in a lump sum at any time you choose, without having to pay the total remaining interest. You might at a future date come into money, enabling you to make such a payment. Or you may wish to pay off your terms with the developer in order to resell the property.

Developers often offer excellent terms to purchasers who begin their payments before the building is finished. This can be favourable to the buyer, but he must be sure that the developer is reliable and solvent, and can bring the project to completion.

The developer must offer a bank guarantee which assures the buyer the return of his invested money if the project stalls or fails. An important point is that this bank guarantee will cost the buyer a small percentage of the price. It is a separate transaction with the bank, not necessarily included in all contracts. If the developer offers this guarantee, details must be clearly spelled out, either in the contract or in a separate document.

Spanish consumer legislation requires that all contracts spell out terms clearly. Do not be afraid to ask plenty of questions. And use a Spanish lawyer.

BANK LOANS AND MORTGAGES

With the introduction of the euro and the lifting of almost all exchange controls, both residents and non-residents may now obtain loans and mortgages against their Spanish property in any currency from any bank in the world — if they can find a bank willing to lend against property in another country. Even very long-term endowment mortgages are beginning to appear, offered by Spanish branches of UK lending institutions.

The good news is the inflation and interest rates are at an all-time low in Spain. Spanish bank mortgages are now being offered at rates of less than four per cent, the lowest in Europe. Signs for 2006 are that rates should continue low. The euribor, the base lending rate for the euro, rises a little and then falls a little, staying at bottom levels.

Those people purchasing a second home in Spain may find they can obtain a mortgage property in their home country for the purchase of property in Spain. This could represent an ideal solution, but UK residents in particular must be careful about losing tax relief when they mortgage to purchase outside the UK.

SUBSIDISED HOUSING

In Spain, as in most countries, the government subsidises some types of housing. Ordinarily, this housing is destined for the poor and is offered to them on favourable terms.

Such housing is known in Spain as V.P.O., or *Vivienda de Protección Oficial*. You may think that this housing is not meant to help well-to-do foreigners purchase vacation homes, and you would be right. But there are several classes of V.P.O. projects. One class, operated by the Spanish government, is available only to the poor, who must make a declaration of poverty in order to obtain it.

The other class, more frequently seen, is based on the provision of cheap government financing to the project developer, and these apartments are available to foreigners, although controls are becoming stricter. Purchasers must be residents and they cannot have incomes of more than about 1,500 a month.

Nevertheless, especially if you are an EU citizen and an official resident of Spain, earning a living here, with a modest income, you may qualify for government assistance in buying your home, just as Spaniards do.

Remember, when purchasing V.P.O. flats, the offer will stipulate that you make a very small down payment, but if you can make a larger payment of 20,000 or so, and thus totally clear the constructor's own financial contribution to the project, this will be very advantageous. The balance, payable over 15 years or more on favourable terms, will then repay only the cheap government loan and not contribute further to the constructor's profit.

There are, of course, controls on the resale of such flats, which block speculators profiting at the expense of the government.

INSURING YOUR HOME

As in any country, it is sound practice to carry homeowner's insurance protecting you against damage to the building itself, damage or theft of its contents, and against claims from others who may suffer injury or damage resulting from your ownership.

This is especially important when you are absent from your Spanish property for long periods, but be alert to clauses in your contract which render your insurance invalid if you are away from the property for more than a stated period of time. Often, by paying an extra premium, you can be covered even though you are absent much of the time.

Both Spanish and international insurers offer various policies at various prices. Make enquiries among older residents to find a company which has given good service.

As in most countries, you fill out a form in which you put a value you wish to insure on your house and its contents. Remember that, should you choose to insure your property for only half its real value, the insurance company, which makes its own evaluation, will pay you only half the value of any individual items which are stolen or damaged. People sometimes think they can insure half and then get full value when only two or three items are stolen or damaged, but this is not so.

The company will also ask you to report on whether your property will be unoccupied for lengthy periods, how old the building is, how many doors and windows there are, whether they are guarded by iron-barred *rejas,* if there is a burglar alarm system, and so on. If you do not respond truthfully to these questions, there can be grounds for a later denial of any claim you make. Your premiums will vary according to your situation.

Be sure to read the fine print in your policy. Often, insurance against theft of the contents of your property will not pay unless entrance has been forced and there is evidence for this. If a "guest" at one of your parties makes off with your wife's jewels, you will not be paid. If there is no copy of the contract available in your language, have someone translate for you.

What will insurance cost you? Policies and conditions vary, but you can estimate that about one euro per year per thousand euros of value will cover the building itself against damage by natural causes or fire or explosions, if the building is located in a town. An older house in the country, far from fire-fighting services, would cost more to insure.

Insurance of your furniture and household effects will be somewhere around   2.50 per thousand euros of value if you live in an apartment; up to   3.50 per thousand if you live in a detached villa. This covers fire and theft.

If one of your steps collapses and the postman breaks his leg, or you leave the bathtub water running until your downstairs neighbour's apartment is flooded, they can claim compensation from you as the owner. You can cover yourself for claims up to   50,000 for less than   20 a year

Most Spanish companies offer a comprehensive policy covering the building, the contents and third party claims. One company quoted a figure of   1,200 per year for comprehensive coverage of a villa and contents valued at   240,000. An apartment or townhouse would be less costly.

TIMESHARE LAW

A comprehensive Spanish law regulates important legal aspects of timeshare itself and provides consumer protection that brings the country into line with European timeshare regulations.

Putting a crimp into the high-pressure selling techniques of the timeshare touts around bus stations and tourist spots, the law provides a 10-day cooling-off period during which no deposit may be taken and the buyer can withdraw from the contract he has signed without any penalty.

Furthermore, the law requires that the timeshare operator provide full information and a contract in the buyer's own language. If any element of the purchase does not meet the brochure or written description or match the contract terms, the buyer has a further three months to rescind the contract unilaterally with no penalty.

The law also provides that any loan which the buyer may have taken out to purchase the timeshare will also be cancelled. This has been one tricky aspect of hard sales, in which the timeshare seller offers a low-interest loan to the prospective buyer. All well and good, but if the buyer later wants out of his contract, he finds that he still owes the loan to the bank, a third party, and it must be paid off. This practice is ended by the new law.

The law also provides that all contracts will be subject to Spanish law. That is, even if the buyer's contract states that its terms are subject to the laws of some distant offshore jurisdiction, where the timeshare company's headquarters are located, this provision is not valid and the contract will be subject to interpretation in Spanish courts.

This has been a thorny point in many timeshare contracts because the buyers found it difficult to dispute any point when the court was thousands of miles away.

Even the service companies which maintain the resorts have, until now, often been registered in offshore tax havens. This made it difficult for timeshare buyers to bring action against the companies when they failed to keep the resorts in good condition.

Under terms of Spain's new law, the service companies must have a permanent establishment registered inside Spain, where they can be held legally responsible.

Furthermore, the new law makes the resort owner finally responsible for proper maintenance of the resort, and action can be taken against the resort owner if the service company fails to perform.

On the other hand, the resort operator can repossess an owner's holiday weeks if the owner fails to pay one year's maintenance charges. The operator must give 30 days certified notice before he can do this, and, unless this right is specifically renounced in your contract, he must pay back the owner the value of his remaining weeks in the scheme.

That is, a timeshare plan may run from a minimum of three years to a maximum of 50 years. If an owner has used his weeks for 25 years in a 50-year plan, and then defaults, the operator must pay him back half of his original price, as well as assuming the debt owed by the owner to the service company.

However, it is also possible for the timeshare contract to contain a penalty clause which will let the company keep the entire amount originally paid. Watch out for this clause in your timeshare contract.

The law also provides that timeshare contracts can be registered in Spain's Property Registry as a special right, although the law is also very careful to note that timeshare is not a property right as such, that it is a service contract not a property sale.

The full name of the law in fact is The Law Regulating the Rights of Rotational Enjoyment of Real Estate for Touristic Use, and it forbids any mention of property rights in timeshare publicity.

Unfortunately, the law does not mean that all timeshare sales are now regulated and controlled to protect the consumer. Timeshare companies have already come up with new schemes relating to "vacation plans" and "point systems" to move their products out of the area controlled by the law.

EXPROPRIATION OF PROPERTY

For most people, any improvement of the road system or flyovers and bypasses to increase safety is good news.

It may not be such good news if your property borders a projected highway or is affected by a new bypass, because the authorities — represented by a public works department such as the *Ministerio de Obras Públicas y Transportes* or MOPT — can expropriate your property and put you off it.

They must pay you, of course. The doctrine of *justiprecio* applies, meaning they must pay you a fair price. You may have to fight them to get it, however.

There are legal avenues open to you to protect your rights in the matter.

First, the authorities must officially inform you that expropriation proceedings are about to begin against you. They will send you an official letter inviting you to attend the *acta previa a la ocupación*. This is a hearing, usually held in your town hall, at which you may present any protest you have about the extent of your property being expropriated.

Money is not discussed at this first hearing, only the amount of land being taken. You should take skilled legal counsel with you when you go to this hearing.

If the authorities are only interested in a few square metres of your vast finca, then you have no real problem. If, however, they want to put the road through the kitchen and reception area of your popular restaurant, or if the amount of land they take will leave you with too few square metres to be buildable, then there must be some negotiating.

In such a case, some lawyers advise that you attempt to make the authorities expropriate your *entire* property and not just part of it. This obviously is because the property, once divided, becomes all but worthless and such a situation is manifestly unfair to the person involved.

In these negotiations, the authorities are usually reasonable and fair, but they will be even more fair and reasonable when confronted by skilled counsel.

Your chances of resisting expropriation altogether are very poor indeed. The entire concept of expropriation or Eminent Domain exists because sometimes the public good takes precedence over private ownership. They are going to build the highway and your chance of moving the route away from your private property is very small.

Once the amount of land being expropriated is agreed, the authorities take the situation under analysis and then communicate their offer of payment to each owner. If the offer is acceptable, you inform them and the deal is done.

If, however, as is more frequent, you are not satisfied with their offer, you negotiate again. The doctrine of *justiprecio* is not just a word and it can be enforced. You will need to prepare a case for a higher price on your property, including sales prices of land around you, improvements you have made, and so on. You will need expert advice for this.

If you are unable to come to an agreement with the authorities by negotiation, you have recourse to the *Jurado de Expropiaciones*, which is a special court set up for this purpose only. The presiding members of this tribunal are not only judges; real estate experts are also included, and decisions it has rendered have ensured that fair market value is paid to many owners.

Beyond that, you can appeal this tribunal's ruling to the normal courts all the way up to the Supreme Court.

To sum up, in any expropriation proceedings, you have little chance of resisting entirely the order. But you do have two opportunities to protest both the amount of land being taken and the payment offered. Skilled counsel can make sure your interests are protected.

GLOSSARY

Abogado – Lawyer, solicitor

Administrador de Fincas – Licensed professional property administrator

API – **Agente de la Propiedad Inmobiliaria** – Real estate agent, member of long-established association.

Arbitrio sobre el incremento del valor de los terrenos – Municipal tax on property sales, see *Plus Valía*.

Boletín Oficial – Official State gazette, where laws are published

Catastro – Land Office, concerned with measurements and physical description

Certificado Catastral – Catastral certificate describing land and buildings

Comunidad de Propietarios – Community of Property Owners

Declaración de Obra Nueva – Declaration of new construction

Escritura de Compraventa – Sales contract

Escritura Pública – Registered title deed

Expediente de Dominio – Ownership Proceeding, to establish title

Finca – Any plot of land or property

Gestor – Licensed administrative expert in Spanish procedures

GIPE – *Gestor y Intermediario de Propiedades y Edificios,* title awarded by association of estate agents and property administrators.

Hipoteca – Mortgage

Impuesto sobre Bienes Inmuebles (IBI) – Annual real estate tax

Impuesto de Transmisiones Patrimoniales (ITP) – Property transfer tax

Jurado de Expropiaciones – Special tribunal for expropriations

Justiprecio – Doctrine of fair price by the State in forcible purchase

Ley de Costas – Shores Act, protecting coastline

Ley de Tasas – Law of public fees

Ministerio de Obras Públicas y Transportes (MOPT) – Ministry of Public Works and Transport

Nota Simple – Certificate of registration from Property Registry

Plan General de Ordenación Urbana (PGOU) – Town development plan

Plan Parcial – Plan of building plots on urbanisation

Plus Valía – Municipal tax on property sale

Poder – Power of attorney

Registro de la Propiedad – Property Registry

Reja – Iron grillwork protecting windows and doors

Reposesión – Repossessed property

Subasta – Auction

Subasteros – Professional auction buyers

Topógrafo – Property surveyor

Urbanismo – Town planning department

Valor Catastral – Assessed value of property for tax purposes

2.   SELLING YOUR PROPERTY

Now is still a good time to sell your Spanish property. In most areas the red-hot boom has cooled off but prices continue to rise steadily and demand from northern Europeans is brisk.

Sellers should be aware, however, that they are subject to Spanish capital gains tax on the profits from their sale, whether they are resident or non-resident.

Furthermore, a sale of Spanish property attracts transfer costs that can total as much as 20 per cent of the price, in addition to that capital gains tax.

In some areas, real estate agents charge commissions of 10 per cent, although the Spanish estate agents' association recommends 3 per cent. Add to this taxes and costs that total about 10 per cent and you are looking at some very high transfer costs.

Non-residents pay capital gains tax at a flat rate of 35 per cent on their profit from the sale. The Spanish Tax Agency requires that a buyer from a non-resident withhold 5 per cent of the price and pay it directly to the tax agency. Residents pay a maximum of 15 per cent, with the tax calculated as part of their income tax. They are not subject to the withholding of 5 per cent.

You may be exempt from capital gains in three cases.

You originally bought your property before 1987.

You are 65 years old, a resident, and you have lived in your home for a minimum of three years.

You are resident and you use the full purchase price to buy another principal residence in Spain.

For full details on taxes involved in selling property, see the following section, Taxes on Property.

PROPERTY SELLER'S CHECKLIST

1. ESTATE AGENT

First, read the section on estate agents in the previous chapter, Buying Property.

One rule often cited by those who have sold their homes in Spain is: Don't try to do it yourself. Get an estate agent, or several, and let them handle the showing of the place and dealing with prospects. Otherwise, you go crazy. There may be exceptions to this rule, but most sellers are in agreement.

Very seldom do Spanish estate agents demand the exclusive right to market your property, so you will probably list your sale with several agents in your area. Each agent will have his own form of agreement with you, in which his commission is stated if he brings the client who eventually buys your property. This agreement will contain the commission charged. Some agents charge as high as 10 per cent. Five per cent is more frequent. You make your own deal on this.

An agent can help you get your price right. Because of the incredible boom, many owners think they can get a very high price. The market is a little slower today. Your agent will know what the market is in your area. You can then decide if you want to put a higher price and wait longer to sell, or a lower price in order to attract an immediate buyer. Be warned that an agent will not work very hard to market your property if he thinks it is overpriced and unlikely to sell.

A good estate agent will see you through the entire process of finding a buyer, negotiating the price, making the contract, securing the payment, signing before the notary, paying the necessary taxes, and all the other details that arise.

The usual sequence is:

1. Seller and buyer to agree all the details of the purchase on what is called a "private contract", at which time the buyer makes a substantial deposit, usually 10 per cent.

2. This deposit takes your property off the market and holds it while the buyer assembles the full amount of the purchase price, either from his own resources or by obtaining a mortgage. If the buyer does not complete the sale, he loses his deposit. If you, the seller, accept a higher offer in the meantime, you have to return double the amount of the deposit. Be warned. It is astonishing how often an apparently serious purchaser is unable to come up with the cash. Don't count your chickens before they have hatched. Be warned also that many buyers will try to make stage payments and get possession. If they do not complete the payments, you will have plenty of trouble getting them out and recovering your property. (See section below on Lawyers).

3. When the two parties are ready to complete the sale, they go to the Spanish *Notario* and sign the sales contract at his office. The contract can also be signed by proxy. This often happens with an absentee seller. He gives his lawyer a power of attorney, called a *poder* in Spanish. This *poder* empowers the attorney to sign in the name of his client. A seller who does not wish to return to Spain can even make this proxy at the Spanish consulate in his own country. (See Power of Attorney section in Buying Property chapter).

4. This sales contract is stamped by the *Notario* and it should be immediately taken to the Property Registry office, where it is converted into the famous *escritura* − the title deed. The contract is called an *escritura de compraventa,* a purchase contract, and the title

deed is called an *escritura pùblica,* because it is a registered document of public record. They are exactly the same document, before and after its registration. The original deed is then kept at the notary's office. You yourself never have it. You have only an official copy.

It is only this public deed that makes the buyer the new owner, with a title proof against all comers. Discuss the entire procedure step by step with your agent, so you know what is going on at each stage.

The steps listed above are the most usual form of property transactions, but there are many possible variations. If your buyer has the cash ready and you have your title deed clear, there is no reason why you cannot go directly to the Notary and complete the sale immediately, for example.

Don't forget that you want a proper bill – *factura* – from your estate agent, listing the amount of the commission and adding 16 per cent IVA to this sum. Make this clear at the beginning of the transaction. The entire amount is deductible from your profit as a legitimate expense when you go to calculate your capital gains tax if you re-sell the property.

2. LAWYER
Conventional wisdom says that the buyer always needs a lawyer but the seller may not. We say that the seller, in the complex world of international property transfer, really ought to have a lawyer, too. Your estate agent may be perfectly competent, but complications can arise outside his area of expertise. It is always good to have two people working for you as well so you can compare and contrast their views.

For example, some "buyers" will make you an offer of renting with option to buy but their sole intention is getting a cheap rental. They pay you a low rent, and then they stop paying the rent altogether, and then they leave. They had no intention ever of buying the place. And it isn't worth the expense for you to try to collect the last three or four months of rent that they didn't pay, even if you could find them. Furthermore, your property has been off the market for six months or a year.

So, when the term of option to buy is mentioned, you or your lawyer or your estate agent should be aware that it ought to mean that the buyer pays you   10,000 or   15,000 for this option, which will be deducted from the total price when they purchase. If they let the time limit of the option expire, which might be two or three months, they forfeit what they have paid for it.

In spite of our dire warnings throughout this book, the majority of property transfers are quite clear-cut and no problems arise. Very few turn into nightmares. So, lawyer's fees vary widely. You can take one per cent of the purchase price as a guideline for a standard property transfer. Get this clear with your lawyer before you even start. Ask him how much he will charge you. Your legal fees are also deductible from your profits as a necessary expense in realising your capital gain. Again, you need a bill with Spanish IVA charged at 16 per cent.

2. CONTRACT

Your lawyer will also explain to you some things not expressed specifically in the contract.

For example, your contract may state that your buyer pays 50,000 now and takes possession of the property, paying another 30,000 after three months and another 30,000 after an additional three months to complete a total price of 110,000. If he fails to meet any payment, he forfeits the amount already paid and the property returns to you. He promises to vacate immediately. You don't like the idea of the stage payments, but you feel safe because of this clause in your contract.

Your lawyer will warn you that this clause is not strictly enforceable and matters will not turn out so easily if the buyer fails to complete payment. If the buyer can't pay and refuses to leave, you will have to go to court to resolve your contract and get your property back. It will not happen automatically.

The court will probably rule that you indeed get your property back, but that you can't keep all of the money the buyer has already paid you. After the court makes its own calculation of how long the buyer has been in the house, plus inconvenience to you, and a series of other factors, it will decide that you can keep, say, half of the money already paid. Then, after this procedure has dragged out for months, you can again take possession of the property and start again on the process of selling it. This is only one of the many, many complications that come up in property transactions.

Some other points you want to study beforehand will be the division of payment of the transfer taxes and fees. Will you follow Spanish regulations and charge the notary and the *plus valía* tax to the seller and the transfer tax and the registration fee to the buyer? Or will you try to make the buyer responsible for all charges in the transfer? What price will you declare, the real price or a lower figure? (See below for more details on these questions).

49

A good contract will help you foresee and avoid some of these complications but even the best contract cannot protect you against every eventuality. The standard contract used by your estate agent is probably as good as any, but your lawyer may have suggestions to make in your own particular case.

4. DECIDE HOW MUCH TO DECLARE

It was formerly a common practice in Spain to declare a property sale at much lower than its real price, in order to save money on transfer tax and wealth tax later. Since the enactment of the law on public fees, which makes an under-valuation of 20 per cent punishable by surcharges, and since the tax ministry's stricter application of all the rules, this practice has largely ceased. If Hacienda believes that your sale is undervalued — and they have their own tables of market values — they may send you a notice that your sale has been re-assessed by them, along with a bill for how much extra tax you owe. Today, most contracts are declared at their real value. Furthermore, as buyers become more sophisticated, they have realised that a low declaration now means that they will show a larger profit on paper when they go to sell later, making them subject to a higher Spanish capital gains tax.

If you want to know exactly how much Hacienda thinks your property is worth, you can find out by asking at your regional *oficina liquidadora*. They will give you the amount listed in their own tables. Any attempt to declare a value under that figure will probably bring you a notice to pay more.

Furthermore, if Hacienda reckons that the under-declaration exceeds 20 per cent of their calculated value of the property, they can bill you, the seller, for an unjustified capital gain, which draws tax at 35 per cent for the non-resident.

That is, if you declare the sale at   90,000, but Hacienda calculates the market value of the property at   120,000, they will charge the seller 35 per cent of   30,000, or more than   10,000. In addition, they can assume the buyer has received a gift worth   30,000 and assess gift tax on him of about   6,000.

5. ASSEMBLE YOUR DOCUMENTS

It will help your sale to go smoothly if you have all your documents in order before you even begin to advertise. It builds confidence in the possible buyer — and his own lawyer — to see all the right papers in order when they consider purchasing. Here is our suggested seller's kit.

Escritura Pública — The most basic paper of all is your title deed, which shows that you are the registered owner of record with an incontestable title. In fact, you have probably never seen your real title deed. What you have is an authorised copy. Unlike some systems of property registration, in Spain it is not the piece of paper itself which counts; it is the inscription in the *Registro de la Propiedad,* the property registry office. If you lose your deed, you can always get another copy from the Notary, where it is on file permanently. Listed on the inscription in the property registry are any liens, charges or mortgages against the property. Back taxes, however, are not listed. Your prospective purchaser will get for himself a *nota simple* from the registry, which is an extract showing the basic information and any charges against the property, but he will want to look at your copy of the full deed in any case.

In a few cases, owners have their property only on a private contract and the house may not even be registered. If this includes you, don't panic. This can be solved in various ways, depending on the individual circumstances. You can offer your buyer the possibility of a Regulation 205 procedure or a full-scale *expediente de dominio,* (see reference in previous chapter) in which a court will study the case, publish the proceedings, and finally issue a clear title to the property. You might even find a new buyer willing to run the same risks as you in order to avoid taxes, who will simply purchase the property on a new private contract.

IBI Receipt — Your receipt for the paid-up *Impuesto sobre Bienes Inmuebles,* the Real Estate Tax, is an important item. The IBI receipt shows first that the estate tax is paid for this year. It would be a good idea to have the receipts for the last five years, to show good faith. The IBI receipt also shows the amount of the *valor catastral,* the official assessed value of the property for tax purposes. This value is almost always less than the real market value, but they are gradually being raised. The IBI receipt also confirms that the house exists and is registered for taxes, which can be an important point when no *escritura pública* exists and the owner holds the property only by virtue of a private contract. Finally, the IBI must be presented when you sign the contract at the Notary because it also displays the number of the *referencia catastral,* which, since 1997, is a required part of the documentation in property transfers.

Referencia Catastral — The Catastral Reference is the file number of the property's registration in the land registry, which in Spanish is called the *catastro,* a word that exists but is rarely used in English, and which means the land registry. Property is registered here by its measurements and boundaries and physical characteristics. The Property Registry is concerned with ownership and mortgages. You are right if you think that it doesn't make sense to have two separate bodies — which don't even talk to each other — dealing with land and property registration. Now, even the Spanish authorities begin to agree with you and, as a first step, they require that the catastral reference number accompany any property transfer. Furthermore, the Notary and the Property Registry office are now authorised to make note of the fact if there is any great difference in the physical description of the property given in the *catastro* and the legal description given in the sales contract and title deed. This difference might include the fact that the *catastro* shows a four-bedroom villa and a swimming pool while the sales contract mentions only a plot of land at a very low price. It is yet to be seen just how effectively the Notary and the Registrar of Property will inform the tax office, but the way is now clear, so be warned.

It is a good idea for the seller to obtain the completely detailed *Certificado Catastral* and include it in his documentation. This will add to the prospective purchaser's confidence, and will make it absolutely clear what he is buying. Land descriptions on title deeds are often quite vague, even misleading. The *catastro* is usually more accurate, because they have been updating their information for some years now, sending inspectors to check the physical reality of land and houses, and using aerial photographs as well. There are in fact two certificates, a written description and a graphic one, showing the plan of the land. It can take several months to obtain the certificates. There is a small fee.

Income Tax Declaration — If you are a resident, and so not subject to the retention of five per cent of the price, you will be required to present your most recent income tax declaration when you sign the contract at the Notary. The income tax declaration is as important as the residence permit in proving your tax status in Spain.

If you are a non-resident, the buyer may want to see your current Form 214, on which you declare each year for the same property owner's income tax as well as Spanish wealth tax. Non-residents must pay wealth tax because they do not have the exemption of   108,000 that residents have. Non-residents should be warned that any unpaid property owner's income tax or wealth tax can be taken by the tax man from the five per cent retention.

Consult the chapter on Taxes on Property for discussion on how to calculate your capital gains tax on the sale, and the annual taxes on property that you pay every year.

Non-Residence Certificate — This belongs to the buyer, not to the seller, but be warned that, if the buyer is a non-resident and the form of payment is not through a bank cheque which identifies the buyer as the issuer, along with his bank, the buyer must obtain beforehand a certificate of non-residence from the Spanish Ministry of the Interior, and it can take as long as two months for this certificate to be issued.

If payment takes place abroad, for example, by transfer from the buyer's account in London to your own account in London, this is perfectly legal, but it offers the Spanish tax man no control over the transaction for documentation purposes. So, they require this certificate. If the buyer works through a Spanish bank, he will have a certificate of changing the foreign money into euros for property purchase, and Spain can document the transaction. If the sale takes place in pounds outside Spain, this is perfectly legal and acceptable as long as the cheque is presented when the deal is completed at the Spanish notary. It is only when the buyer himself wishes to keep the details anonymous and confidential that he must present the certificate of non-residence. Spain wants to know where the money comes from.

Taxes and Fees — We have discussed in the chapter on Buying Property the two taxes and two fees on property sales.

The two taxes are the ITP — the property transfer tax of 6 or 7 per cent depending on which Region, — and the *plus valía,* a sort of artificial capital gains tax charged by the town hall on the increase in an official set of values for the property. There is also a documents fee of one half of one per cent.

The *plus valía* varies widely, depending on the amount of time that has passed between sales, as we mentioned earlier. You can find out exactly how much it will be by asking at your town hall. They have a *plus valía* office which will tell you the exact amount of the tax beforehand.

The two fees are for the Notary and the Property Registry. They will be in the neighbourhood of   500 but can be higher on large transactions. You can find out exactly how much by asking in advance.

If you determine the amount of these taxes and fees on your sale price in advance, you can include them in your sales presentation kit, which will impress the buyer and his lawyer with your professional approach.

Community charges and statutes — If you are selling a flat or townhouse that belongs to a Community of Property Owners, you will want to include your last bill for the *cuota* — the community yearly charge, along with a copy of the Statutes that regulate your community.

The buyer will want to know what the yearly charge is and he will want to see the Statutes of the community he is joining. It would be a good idea to have a copy of the minutes of the last Annual General Meeting as well, to prove to your prospective purchaser that your community is well run and a nice place to live.

Service bills — Copies of your bills for rubbish, water, electricity and even telephone are necessary parts of your sales presentation. Any buyer will want to know how much these charges are on the property, and he will also want to be sure that they are paid up.

Once you have assembled all this paperwork, it would be a good idea to prepare a folder with photocopies of each relevant document, so that you or your lawyer or your estate agent will be prepared to answer any question that a prospective buyer might have.

GLOSSARY

Abogado – Lawyer, solicitor

Administrador de Fincas – Licensed professional property administrator

API – **Agente de la Propiedad Inmobiliaria** – Real estate agent, member of long-established association.

Arbitrio sobre el incremento del valor de los terrenos – Municipal tax on property sales, see *Plus Valía.*

Catastro – Land Office, concerned with measurements and physical description

Certificado Catastral – Catastral certificate describing land and buildings

Comunidad de Propietarios – Community of Property Owners
Contrato – Contract

Escritura de Compraventa – Sales contract

Escritura Pública – Registered title deed

Factura – Bill

Finca – Any plot of land or property

Gestor – Licensed administrative expert in Spanish procedures

GIPE – *Gestor e Intermediario de Promociones y Edificaciones,* title awarded by association of estate agents and property administrators.

Hipoteca – Mortgage

Impuesto sobre Bienes Inmuebles (IBI) – Annual real estate tax

Impuesto de Transmisiones Patrimoniales (ITP) – Property transfer tax

IVA (Impuesto sobre el Valor Añadido) – Spanish value added tax, charged when developer sells new property to first buyer.

Ley de Costas – Shores Act, protecting coastline

Ley de Tasas – Law of public fees

Nota Simple – Certificate of registration from Property Registry

Notario – Notary

Oficina Liquidadora – Tax office which sets values and collects tax.

Plan General de Ordenación Urbana (PGOU) – Town development plan

Plan Parcial – Plan of building plots on urbanisation

Plus Valía – Municipal tax on property sale

Poder – Power of attorney

Registro de la Propiedad – Property Registry

Tasación – Evaluation of property

Tasador – Property surveyor, evaluator

Topógrafo – Property surveyor

Urbanismo – Town planning department

Valor Catastral – Assessed value of property for tax purposes

3.   BUILDING YOUR OWN HOUSE

If you intend to build your own castle in Spain, the first item on your list should be finding a good lawyer.

This may sound backwards, but when you check out the list below of all the things that can go wrong with buying property, getting a building permit, and contracting the construction, perhaps you will agree.

The second item on your list should be a promise to yourself that you are prepared to put a lot of your own time into overseeing the entire project, from beginning to end. Getting what you want depends on your own personal supervision. Most building projects go up just as planned, with only minor setbacks, but it is best to be prepared and take care before you start.

So, let's suppose that you are determined to buy land and build your dream house. More foreigners than ever are doing this today because of the shortage of quality ready-made villas, and more builders and architects than ever are ready to help you realise your dream. The rewards are great. But be prepared for plenty of exasperation and, above all, don't leap in with your eyes shut.

Too often, the aspiring house-builder thinks that all he has to do is pick one model of villa from a selection that the developer or builder shows him, and that it will appear as if by magic a few months later.

Sometimes this method works out perfectly well, but not all of us can read a plan and visualise the final result with accuracy. Too many people tell their builder that House Type B suits them very well, pay a fat deposit, and go back to their native country. When they return six or eight months later, they find that House Type B doesn't look anything like they thought it would; that the builder hasn't placed it in the spot they had agreed on and, furthermore, they absolutely hate the yellow tiles in the bathroom.

It will take your personal supervision to get it done the way you want it. With forethought and patient attention to detail, you can indeed have your dream house. But let me repeat that first warning. You simply cannot walk away and expect to return finding that your house has been built just the way you want it. You will have to be there every day. Let me repeat. Every day.

First, however, you have to find the land. Everything mentioned in the previous chapter about buying property applies here, and there is more besides.

Building plots with all services are available on many urbanisations, as housing estates are called. Country land, however, has become a problem in most areas. In Andalusia strict enforcement of recent land laws has all but halted new building on country land. On the Costa Blanca, abusive application of the "land-grab law" has made new buyers extremely wary. See the Land Law section below for more detail.

Let's suppose that you have searched through the countryside and found a piece of land you like, or that you have seen a dozen urbanisations and finally chosen a plot.

BUILDING PERMIT

The first thing you have to know is, can you get permission from the town hall to build on it? The permit is called *licencia de obra* or *permiso de obra*. Be advised that building permits cost around four per cent of the estimated construction cost. This can vary from town to town. And the town hall clearance is not the end of the story. The Housing Department of each Region, like Andalusia or Valencia, oversees building and it must vet and clear each application as well. It sometimes happens that a town hall is happy to issue a building licence but the Regional authorities then block it. You need to have approval of both bodies.

URBAN LAND

If your land is in a registered urbanisation, or housing estate, with its papers in order, you will probably have no problem. Sometimes the land comes with the building permit already arranged. This land, of course, is more expensive because it has been prepared for development. But even on a registered urbanisation, problems can arise.

There are zoning changes from time to time, and you may find your beautiful property is in the middle of a green zone where no building can take place. You may find that your urbanisation was started a few years ago under dubious permits issued in the building boom and today's strict enforcement of laws has paralysed further building. This is why you need expert legal advice.

DO NOT believe the seller. Your town hall's *urbanismo* department is a very important stop for you. Go yourself and take someone who speaks Spanish. Your lawyer, for example.

PGOU: You want to see the PGOU, the *Plan General de Ordenación Urbana,* the Town Plan. These plans generally are approved every four years. Any interim changes in them must be publicly posted and approved, with a chance for affected property owners to protest or make claims.

In many municipalities, you may find that changes have been made in the building codes and Town Plans, sometimes approved by the town hall but still needing the final go-ahead from the regional government, which must vet and clear the municipal plans.

In some cases, there are special building codes set up for specific zones. The PGOU analysis is not for amateurs. You need a specialist to make sure you understand it. If your land is located in an existing and approved urbanisation, the permit will probably be forthcoming, but you must still check on it. You must also be sure that the urbanisation is an approved one.

There are some developments that never received official approval and where building is stopped today because they never met the legal requirements for the services they must provide, such as roads of a certain width, or water supply. You can find out by asking to see the *proyecto de urbanización* and the *plan parcial,* or the plan of parcels, building plots, at the town hall.

Be sure to check also the building regulations for plots and areas around your chosen spot. One of the worst, and most frequent, horror stories on the fast-growing coasts of Spain is the nightmare of the cut-off view. That is, you return to your pleasant villa on a hillside overlooking the Mediterranean to discover that a four-storey apartment building now blocks your view, and your new neighbours look right into your bedroom window. Make sure that you know what type of building permits will be issued around you before you buy.

BUILDING COSTS

These costs are very approximate. So many variations come into building costs that it is extremely difficult to calculate an average price that means anything. Nevertheless, the table should give you some idea of what to expect.

Basic Construction: figure 500–600 euros a square metre.

Good Construction: 600-700 euros a square metre

Quality Construction: 900 euros a square metre and up, way up.

BASIC CONSTRUCTION means walls of the large solid building blocks with no cavities and the use of basic flooring and finishing materials.

GOOD CONSTRUCTION at the top end of the price will include cavity walls and some higher quality finishing materials. No air-conditioning or central heating, however, and no marble.

QUALITY CONSTRUCTION: The sky is the limit here. Remember that the area of location is also an influence. Labour costs are higher in Marbella than in the interior, for example.

In the brisk building climate today, this check-up may be more complicated than it sounds.

In some municipalities the urban planning authorities even make special deals with developers, whereby land is re-zoned to permit greater building in exchange for part of the builder's profits going into the Town's coffers. This is neither illegal nor corrupt, as the profits help all residents of the town, but it can harm the interests of those who already have purchased.

These special arrangements are called *convenios*, meaning simply "agreements". A wave of protest has arisen in Marbella, for example, where the Town Plan (passed by the town hall but still not finally approved by the Andalusian Regional Government) provides for enormous amounts of new building, enough to triple the population in the next six years.

Current residents charge that some present building permits have been granted for land zoned for parks and schools, and that such rapid new building will lower the quality of life in the town. Be sure to talk with your new neighbours before you sign any contracts.

COUNTRY LAND - *RÚSTICO*

If your land is in the deep country, you will need to check on other factors at the town hall, such as whether you need to buy, say, 10,000 square metres of land, or 30,000 square metres of land, in order to build.

Most country land is zoned as *Rústico,* which means land not programmed for development. It might be farmland or pasture or forest. If building is permitted at all on this type of land, it will be restricted. Regulations vary around Spain, but a typical requirement is that a minimum building plot must be 10,000 square metres if the land has a source of water, and 30,000 square metres if it is zoned as "dry".

Do not believe a seller who tells you that you can build on 6,000 square metres illegally and later have the house registered, paying only a small fine. This has been true in some cases, but most municipalities are now cracking down on such practices. They can order the structure demolished and have done so in some recent cases. Make sure you buy enough land.

You can find this out at the local town hall. The *Urbanismo,* or development, department can tell you exactly what will be permitted or prohibited within any area of the municipality. Visit the town hall yourself, taking someone who speaks Spanish, or send your lawyer, to make absolutely sure that a permit will be forthcoming. And remember that the local permit must be cleared by the Regional land office as well.

The land might have a *camino real* or a *servidumbre de paso,* an old pathway that crosses the land. It is a right of way and you can't cut it by building. People can pass over your land and it might even be transformed into a road some day. Or an irrigation ditch might exist, which again is a legal right of way you cannot block, nor can you deny access to it for those who use it. Country land may have water problems, too. Where does the water come from? Can it be cut off? If you intend to drill your own well, you will need a special permission for this.

Have an expert check the town planning maps to see if any new highways are planned for the zone. It can come as a nasty surprise two years later when you see the bulldozers starting work next door, or you are called to a hearing where expropriation proceedings will start to take the bottom of your garden.

VALENCIA, ANDALUSIA LAWS MAY COMPLICATE MATTERS

Land laws enacted in the Valencian Community and in Andalusia may complicate your land purchase. You must be alert.

In Valencia, the LRAU has country property owners outraged. The initials stand for the *Ley Reguladora de Actividades Urbanísticas,* the Law Regulating Urbanisation Activities. The law provides that town halls may designate private developers as "urbanising agents", with the power to compel private owners either to sell parts of their land at low prices, or to pay high charges for infrastructure.

After massive local protests, involving both Spaniards and foreigners, the European Union sent investigators, who issued a devastating report on Valencia's abuse of basic citizen´s rights.

If you buy in an established urbanisation, you should be all right. If you buy country land or property, make sure your lawyer checks on any possible urbanisation plans in the area.

In Andalusia, the revised *Ley del Suelo,* the Land Law, has some similar provisions, but authorities affirm that more protections are in place to guarantee the rights of private owners. The revised law also cracks down on the practice of illegal construction on *suelo rústico,* or country land. Its main effect has been to virtually halt the sale of country plots, of any size.

LAND MEASUREMENT

Once you have finally determined that a building permit will be forthcoming and that no special encumbrances exist on the land, you can start to find out just what land you are buying.

The seller must have an *escritura*, a title deed, for the land, just as for a flat or land with an existing house. As we mentioned in the preceding chapter, sometimes there is no registered title for the land, only a private document. See the preceding chapter for various ways of getting the land officially registered.

But, in the more usual case where official title exists, this *escritura pública* will describe the land, but sometimes the description isn't exact enough to suit you. Descriptions in the Property Registry often use vague terms like the bare statement that the land borders on the east with the land of Pepe García. Well, Pepe García has a big farm. Just what part of it constitutes the border? It could be where the fence is or where the ditch is or where the path is.

Then you need an official survey. Remember that the Property Registry is concerned with ownership, not with exact description. A surveyor is called a *topógrafo* and he will measure your plot exactly. You can have this done independently but you should also check the Catastral Registry.

CHECK THE CATASTRO

Here again, just as with buying a house, you want to check with the *Catastro* as well as the Property Registry. The Catastral Office lists the boundaries and measurements and physical characteristics of the land. You want to be sure that this description squares with the description in the *escritura*.

If not, you may be able to get the catastral reference to square with the reality of the land, and this in turn with the title deed. The *Catastro* will have a map, a plan of the land, so that you can see that the boundary with Pepe García's farm runs along the fence, just as you might think. Or you might see that your plot includes some triangle of what Pepe García thinks belongs to him. Especially in old country properties, there is often some confusion.

You want to have exact, officially recognised boundaries, and the number of square metres the same on the survey and the *escritura*. They probably will not agree, but you can correct this when you purchase, so that your own title and the physical description are in agreement. This clarity will be greatly to your benefit should you later wish to sell your land and house.

Ask for the official surveyor at the town hall. The survey will form part of your *escritura* when you buy the land. If your land is on an approved urbanisation, there will likely be an up-to-date survey already existing. The survey and the *plan parcial* will also show your access and where your water and electricity come from.

Once you have determined that you can indeed build and you know the exact borders of your land, you had better find out if the seller is in fact the owner of the land. Are you buying from the developers of the urbanisation, or from an individual? If the land is in the *campo,* does Juan really own it? He may share it with his two brothers, one of whom does not want to sell. Or there may be a mortgage on it. The same rules apply as for any property purchase. Check the *Registro de la Propiedad.*

Finally, you sign the *escritura de compraventa* at the *notario,* and you are ready to proceed with building. When you checked restrictions at the town hall, you should also have discovered what building code problems you may have. Do you have to leave three metres between your boundary and any building? Can you put a wall closer to the road than one metre?

ARCHITECT AND LEGAL EXPENSES

Architect Fee: 8 to 9 per cent (Official College says 6 per cent, Try to negotiate)

Aparejador (Building Engineer): 2.8 per cent (he supervises building construction)

Building Licence: 4 to 5 per cent (varies from town to town)

Topographic Land Survey: 0.66 per cent

Safety Study: 0.8 per cent

Geological Report: 0.94 per cent

First Occupation Licence: half of one per cent

Declaration of New Construction: half of one per cent (you pay this when you register the house for taxes)

Total: 16 to 19 per cent

Is two storeys the absolute limit? If you are in an established urbanisation, does the association of property owners require you to submit your building plans for approval?

We repeat that checking the building code sounds simple but in practice it is often complicated. Many municipalities have old building codes in place, with new ones written and approved by the Town Council, but not yet ratified by their Regional Governments, which must give final approval.

This means that even official *permisos de obra*, or building permits, are sometimes granted on the basis of shaky legality. In addition, it is common to find that some zones have special regulations within the main system. You really want an expert with local knowledge to check on this.

BUILDING CAN BE SIMPLE

In spite of the possible problems we have listed above, the building itself might be very easy. Many of the larger urbanisations will put you in touch with two or three building contractors who work regularly with them.

They will show you several models of homes, together with their prices and specifications, all included, from site preparation to curtain selection. You pick out what you want; suggest a few personal needs and changes; agree to payment terms, and then all you need is to check on progress from time to time, and make sure they are giving you what they promised.

This is the easy way. It's a little more expensive, because all this service costs money and even then you have to keep checking up to make sure you are getting what was promised.

But maybe you want a home that you yourself have designed. You sit on the land for a while and you get some ideas. You want a terrace here for the view, and the pool in that fold of land. You want the bedrooms along the back and the living room in the front, facing south to the sea. None of the ready-made designs suit you.

ARCHITECT IS NECESSARY

Now you need an architect. You have your rough sketches but you need someone who can turn them into real blueprints. In fact, you will need architect's drawings in order to get your building permit in any case.

The only way to find a good architect is to ask around. If you prefer to use a foreign architect for your design, you may do so. Since Spain's entry into Europe, EU architects can now practise and sign plans for approval by the official *Colegio de Arquitectos.*

Architects' fees, at least as a minimum, are standard and are set by the *Colegio.* They are about 6 per cent of the estimated cost of construction.To this you must add another 3 per cent for the *aparejador* so your design and supervision will cost you about 9 per cent of your estimated construction cost. This construction cost, by the way, will be less than either your real cost or the real market value of the house when finished.

The price includes final plans that must suit you, and the six copies necessary for approval by the College of Architects and for your building permit. The six and three per cent figures are no longer obligatory, but are only suggested minimum charges, as the College no longer has the legal power to enforce the rates. Hence, you may be able to get a cheaper fee by a little negotiating.

MEMORIA IS BINDING AGREEMENT FOR BUILDING SPECIFICATIONS

The price also includes preparation of the *memoria de calidades,* or building specifications, which includes items like the size of pipes, the formula for the concrete, and the type of materials to be used.

You yourself want to have a personal hand in this. You can choose here just what sort of electrical fittings and bathroom fixtures and kitchen tiles you want. This is the time to think of details about shelves and about whether you want wood window frames or aluminium, and so on.

It is important to give this a great deal of thought because the *memoria* is what you will give your builder in order to get his bid on the job. He will set his price according to the materials stated in the *memoria,* and any changes you may make later, or any additions, will cost you extra. These extras can add up to a lot of money, so the *memoria* is a very important document.

If the builder fails to install any items as set out in these building specifications, he can be held responsible. The architect's fee includes overall supervision of the construction, but you are not likely to see your architect on the building site once he has finished the design.

The actual supervision usually falls to the *aparejador,* a professional architectural engineer who sees that the building is carried out to the specifications required. He will visit the site from time to time to check on things and he will take his own fee, about half what the architect charges you. He signs the documents certifying that the house is properly constructed, which you will need in order to occupy your house legally and to get your electricity connected. Your architect will be able to recommend an *aparejador*. Often they work out of the same office.

Finally, you are ready to find a builder. It is only reasonable to get several bids on your job, remembering that the lowest bid is not always the best deal and that the highest bid does not ensure high quality. Ask around.

Your contract with the builder should include the *memoria*. It should state the total price; whether or not the site grading and preparation and final clean-up are included; the manner of payment, and give a definite completion date, with a penalty clause for late delivery. You ought to have your lawyer vet this contract.

Be advised that many building projects are not finished on time. If your contract contains a penalty clause, well and good. Often, however, the only guarantee is that you can get your money back if the project is not delivered on time.

In real life, you don't want your money back. The apartment or house is already worth 10 or 20 per cent more than you paid for it a year ago, when construction started, so you would suffer this loss.

In this case, you simply wait.

PAYMENT SCHEDULES VARY

Payment terms are not standard, but a typical schedule might be:

1. A deposit of 20 per cent when the contract is signed.
2. Another 20 per cent when the walls and roof are completed. (At this point, it is customary to have the *bandera* party, when a flag is placed on the roof, and the owner invites the workers and his own friends to a fiesta at the site.)
3. Another 20 per cent when the door and window frames are installed and the inside is more or less complete.
4. Another 20 per cent when the house is painted and ready to inhabit, with plumbing and electricity installed and functioning.
5. A payment of 10 per cent when all the outside work included in the contract is finished, such as patios, walls, pool.
6. The final payment of 10 per cent should be held back for six months to a year, if you can swing the deal, to cover any defects in construction which don't show up until the rains start, for example. There is always something.

CONSTRUCTION LAW - LOE

Spain's building law of 2000 makes builders legally responsible for 10 years for any damage resulting from the foundations, load-bearing walls and other structural elements. The builder is responsible for three years for damages caused by construction material defects, and for one year for the state of finishing elements. The law is called the LOE, the *Ley de Ordenación de Edificación*. Architects and builders have been sent to jail in Spain when their buildings collapsed before this period.

Now you have your dream house, but there are still two things you must do. One is to register the house for real estate taxes, the *Impuesto sobre Bienes Inmuebles* (IBI).

DECLARACIÓN DE OBRA NUEVA

However, in order to do this, you must first make a *declaración de obra nueva*, a declaration of new work, in order to have the structure appear on your *escritura*. So far, your deed mentions only the piece of land, not the house you have just built.

The declaration of new construction will cost you one half of one per cent of the declared value of the construction. Again, if the Tax Agency does not agree with your declared value, they can raise it.

Your lawyer or property consultant will show you how to register the new house. If you do not register *(dar de alta)* with the tax people, you can be fined, so take care of it as soon as possible. Two per cent of the value of your house is also calculated as income when you go to file for your Spanish income tax.

When you go to make your declaration of new work and register the house, you will need the *certificado final de obra* issued by the architect, the *licencia de obra*, building permit, issued by the town hall, and the *licencia de primera ocupación*, the permit to inhabit the dwelling, from the town hall.

Then you will be the completely legal and registered owner of your dream house and you can begin to pay both property owner's income tax and Spanish wealth tax on your new property. That is, if you are a non-resident. Residents are exempt from property owner's imputed income tax on their principal dwelling, as well as having the exemption of 108,182 euros on wealth tax.

GLOSSARY

Aparejador – Building engineer

Arquitecto – Licenced Architect

Bandera – Flag, here referring to "flag party" when house is roofed

Camino Real – Royal Road, meaning right of way across land

Catastro – Land Registry, distinct from Property Registry

Escritura de Compraventa – Conveyance Deed

Escritura Pública – Registered title to land

Certificado de Final de Obra – Construction completion certificate

Declaración de Obra Nueva – Declaration of new construction

Ley de Ordenación de la Edificación – Law of Construction

Ley Reguladora de Actividades Urbanísticas – Valencian urbanisation law providing for compulsory purchase

Ley de Suelo – Andalusian land law restricting new building in country areas

Licencia de Obra (Permiso de Obra) – Building Licence

Licencia de Primera Ocupación – Licence to occupy the dwelling

Memoria de Calidades – Detailed building specifications

Plan General de Ordenación Urbana (PGOU) – Municipal building plan

Plan Parcial – Plan of building plots in housing estate

Proyecto de Urbanización – Housing estate development plan

Rústico – country land, not zoned for building

Servidumbre de Paso – Legal right of way

Topógrafo – land surveyor

Urbanismo – Urban Development Office

4. LETTING AND RENTING

BUYING TO LET

The boom in buying to let has slowed in Spain, as it has in the UK, along with a less exuberant property market in general. The slowdown in Spanish property sales and price increases does not mean a crash. The market is still brisk and prices are still rising, but not as quickly as before. This means that a buyer must take extra care to choose the best investment property.

With today's low interest rates and high rentals, you can still, with care, buy a flat on the Costa del Sol, mortgage 70 per cent of the purchase price, and sit back while your rental income pays off the mortgage.

If you pay mortgage interest at under five per cent effective annual rate and your rentals are bringing in a return on capital of seven or eight per cent, you are making a profit of two or three per cent. This doesn't seem like much, but you are doing it with the bank's money, not your own, and you are paying for your property. You also have the use of the property for several months of the year because few holiday lets attract tenants for 12 months of the year.

You also enjoy capital appreciation as your property grows in value. Spanish holiday property prices continue to rise steadily, even if not as rapidly as before, making them a better investment than today's sagging stock market.

Thousands of investors are carrying out this operation right at this moment. And that is in addition to people who do not consider themselves investors, but rent out their Costa property sporadically or regularly to help pay it off until they are ready to retire here.

The rental business has become so popular that visitors to the Costa del Sol who stay either in property they own or in rented villas and flats now outnumber traditional tourists who stay in hotels.

Keep in mind that Spanish tax is due on any income arising in Spain and see the sections later in this chapter on problems, such as sitting tenants, that can come up for landlords.

As of 2005, landlords should also be warned that the Spanish tax agency is watching you. Tenants who make income tax declarations in Spain are now required to list their landlord's name and tax identification number on their income tax declaration form. This enables the tax agency to check the rental payments against the landlord's own tax declaration.

LETTING LAW

Spain's current Law of Urban Lettings, the *Ley de Arrendamientos Urbanos,* went into effect on January 1, 1995, but many renters and letters, especially foreigners, are still unaware of its provisions.

The law brought some good news for those Spanish property owners who are still stuck with sitting tenants under the pre-1985 law, and it also brought good news for tenants who were victims of arbitrary rent rises under the law in force from 1985 to 1995.

The 1995 law ended a maze of contradictory Spanish legislation which made life difficult for tenants and landlords alike and all but ruined the rental property market in Spain.

Two of its main provisions make life easier for both landlords and tenants.

1. The current law ends the forcible extension provision of the 1964 law, which made rental contracts indefinitely renewable by the tenant. The present law allows landlords gradually to raise the old controlled and ridiculously low rents of the 1964 law to market prices today, and, eventually, to recover their own property.

2. The law also provides tenants with more security than the 1985 law stipulated, now obliging landlords to renew residential rental contracts each year for up to five years.

THREE RENTAL SITUATIONS

We must distinguish three possible situations for rentals existing in Spain today, depending on when the original contract was made.

1964-1985: Under the terms of the rental laws in effect from 1964 to 1985 tenants were so protected that landlords gave up in despair and stopped building rental apartments, which led to a critical housing shortage. Almost half a million apartments in Spain are still occupied under this old law, which protected a tenant so strongly that he could pass on his rights to his children and even his grandchildren. Further, his rent could never be raised, or raised only by a small percentage related to the inflation rate.

Would you believe there are almost 500,000 apartments in Spain whose tenants pay less than 50 euros a month? There are buildings in Madrid where the grandchildren of the original tenants are living in spacious flats in prestigious areas, paying rents of five euros a month. Until 1985, the landlord was helpless to do anything about it, even though his real estate tax is 1,500 euros a year and his community fees are another 1,000 euros. Next door, another tenant may be paying 1,200 euros a month for the same type of apartment, having signed his contract after 1985.

73

Some foreign property owners on the Spanish Mediterranean coasts fell into this trap before 1985. Thinking to make a little money on their holiday flat or eventual retirement home, they rented it out, with a contract for some specific time period.

Later they were horrified to discover that their tenants refused to vacate and had become entitled to the forcible extension of their contracts, regardless of the landlord's desire to end the letting and recover his property.

Many landlords chose to leave their apartments empty rather than risk the dangers of a sitting tenant. Landlords refused to repair the crumbling buildings which brought them no profit, and nobody would even think of constructing new rental property.

1985-1995: Revised rental laws passed in 1985 by the Socialist government aimed to remedy this situation in the best capitalist way, by making rental properties good business. The revised law provided that all contracts ended when they said they ended, without provision for forcible extension. The law also ended any restrictions on rent increases. Landlords immediately began to raise rents sharply and to offer short-term contracts with little protection for the tenant. Now it was the tenants who suffered, because they were unwilling to settle into a flat from which they might be evicted in one year's time, or be forced to pay sharp increases.

1995: The 1995 rental law now in force is designed to provide a better balance between the rights and needs of tenants and landlords and to bring at last a final solution to the generations of sitting tenants.

If you are one of the foreign property owners stuck with a sitting tenant, you are now able to recover your property. Don't cheer too loudly, however, because it can take you the tenant's lifetime, plus two years. However, you will be able to raise the rent to a normal level over either five years or 10 years, depending on the tenant's income.

If the tenant earns less than 28,000 euros a year, his rent can be gradually raised to market levels over 10 years. If he earns more than that, his rent can be raised in five years to a market figure.

The old-law tenant still has the right to pass on the apartment to his spouse or children. And they can pass it on to their children, but only for two years. After that, the landlord will at last be able to take possession of his own property. In the meantime, of course, he will have been able to raise the rent to the price levels of today.

Landlords in this position should take legal advice from property specialists in order to make sure they are effectively exercising their rights.

There are a number of legal steps that each landlord must take before he can begin raising his rents, such as citing the tenant to declare his income. If the tenant does not respond, the landlord can then begin raising the rent to bring it to a market level within five years, the faster option.

CONTRACT RENEWABLE UP TO FIVE YEARS

The present law provides that residential contracts, as distinct from short-term holiday lets, are subject to yearly renewals up to five years. Rental contracts are usually made for one year but the law requires that the contract is renewable for a total five-year period of tenancy.

A landlord can offer a contract of two years or three years, but, if the tenant decides that he wants to stay on, this contract is renewable for a total period of five years. If the tenant himself wishes a contract of only two or three years, this is all right. The rent can be revised upward by an inflation factor each year.

At the end of the five years, the landlord can raise the rent as much as he chooses, either for his new tenant or for his existing tenant, if he decides to stay on at the new and higher rent.

DEPOSIT

The current letting law also establishes, for the first time in law, the landlord's right to a deposit as a guarantee against damages. The deposit can be held by an agency independent of both landlord and tenant. This agency will not release the deposit until both parties agree.

The deposit consists of one month's rent for a residential unit and two months' rent for commercial premises. The deposit, called a *fianza*, can be held by the housing department of the regional government. In Andalusia, for example, it is deposited with the *Consejería de la Vivienda* of the Andalusian autonomous government, which has offices in major cities.

EVICTION IS DIFFICULT

For what reasons can a landlord evict a tenant and regain his property? Grounds for eviction include failure to pay the rent (although courts have often ruled that these arrears must exceed six months before any action will be taken), damage to the property, use of the property for immoral purposes, subletting without permission from the owner, and causing a serious nuisance to the neighbours.

In any of these cases, a court order must be obtained against the tenant and many months will pass before you get him out.

Necessary Notification: If you have let your property on a five-year *vivienda* contract (see below) and you wish to take possession yourself at the end of that time, remember that you must officially notify the tenant well before the end of the contract that you do not intend to renew it. If you do not do this correctly, the contract can be regarded as renewed for two years at the same rent.

HOLIDAY RENTALS HAVE SEPARATE RULES

The present law does not affect short-term holiday rental contracts, called *arrienda de temporada*. These holiday contracts do not grant the tenant any right to automatic extension and they require that the tenant vacate when the contract ends.

Foreign property owners can be assured of this legal protection when they let their holiday homes for periods of several months. However, they should still take some care with vetting tenants because the legal procedures for eviction of a tenant who refuses to leave can take more than six months, even when the law is on the landlord's side.

There have been a number of recent cases in which unscrupulous tenants have signed up for holiday rentals, say, for two months, and then simply remained in the apartment without paying any further rent. Four to six months later, the landlord is able to obtain an eviction order, but the tenants have lived rent-free for that period. Even though a court enters a judgement against them for the amount of rent owed, they simply move to another town and repeat the scheme.

LANDLORDS, BE WARY

If you are a property owner and you wish to let your own flat or villa in Spain, or go into the tourist accommodation business, you must be very careful about the terms of your contracts and the quality of your tenants.

The opportunity to pay off your property by letting it looks tempting on paper. It can work out to your entire satisfaction, and in fact it usually does. Nevertheless, many problems arise and you need to be wary.

Tenants may damage your furniture or harm your plumbing and electrical installations. Letting agents may keep your money and allow your apartment to fall into ruin while you are absent.

Or you might fall into the short-term contract trap, when your tenant tries to turn his brief holiday rental into a protected five-year residential let.

In good faith you might rent to a young Spanish man who says he has a six-month work contract in your town, and needs a short-term let. Then he moves in his wife and children, who were not mentioned when he signed the contract, and then he brings in his own furniture.

Then he goes to court to accuse you of coercing him into signing the short-term contract when he really wanted a place to live. As he lives and works in the town, the court will probably rule in his favour, and you will have to wait five years to recover your property.

The safest way is to let only to people you know and trust. Even then it is a good idea to get the rent in advance and a deposit against possible damages as well. Electric bills always arrive late, so it is best to include an estimated charge in the rent. If you have a telephone, you will find that having it disconnected and reconnected is an irritating exercise. But it's worth it. You can get a lock for it, but that is never quite sufficient. Perhaps the best idea is to have the sort of phone which you can unplug from the wall and remove. There have been many problems with telephones.

The property owner who goes into long-term residential letting should also be aware of the residential tenant's right to first refusal if the property is put up for sale. See The Right of First Refusal in the following section on Renting in Spain.

LETTING AGENCIES

If you let your property on a casual basis and for only a few short periods each year, you will probably let by word of mouth to people you know or people recommended by friends.

If you let on a more regular basis, you will probably use an agency or holiday company. You may find that your garden apartment development or your urbanisation office includes a letting service which, for a commission, will handle all the details for you. This could be your solution, but read the agreement carefully and talk to others who have used this service to make sure they are satisfied. Letting commissions run around 15 per cent of the rent.

There are also holiday companies which bring people to Spain for self-catering vacations. These are becoming more popular, so companies are always looking for new properties to let. Because they charge their clients high prices for short stays, they can afford to pay you, the owner, a good price for the use of your property.

Or you might choose to have a real estate agency in Spain handle your lettings. Try to find out if the agency or company is reputable and trustworthy. Talk to other owners to see if they are satisfied with the service.

There have been cases where the agency has rented out the property and told the owner that it was not rented. The agency kept all of the money and the absentee owner assumed that his flat was empty.

Read their contracts with care and pay special attention to clauses concerning compensation in the case of damage to your property. If you make long lets through an agency, make sure that your letting agent is not empowered to sign extensions of contracts or to make new contracts without your knowledge and consent.

Also make sure that this company is legally registered and that it is paying all the proper taxes. Because, when you provide linens and other hotel-type services, and deal with many tourist visitors on a short-term basis, you move into a new area legally. You are now a business yourself and in many tourist areas of Spain, you should legally declare your property as a tourist letting accommodation.

NON-RESIDENT RENTAL TAX

It is quite legal and proper for you, as either a resident or non-resident property owner in Spain, to rent out your property. Be advised, however, that you must declare your rental income for Spanish income tax.

Even if your tenant pays you in British pounds before he leaves for Spain, legally this income arises in Spain because the property is in Spain. It is almost certainly true that most owners who let their property occasionally say nothing about it to the tax authorities and the chances of their getting caught are slim.

Nevertheless, Spanish income tax is due on any profits arising in Spain. If you are a non-resident, you are liable for Spanish non-resident income tax of 25 per cent from the very first euro of rental income, declared on form 210.

If you are a resident, you should add your rental income to your other income when you make your annual Spanish income tax declaration. You can also take advantage of Spain's 50 per cent tax reduction for landlords who let. Non-residents cannot do this.

If you are renting your property on a regular basis to short-term holidaymakers and providing hotel-type services, you must register your property as a tourist letting accommodation, which means inspectors will come to check on your standards.

RENTING IN SPAIN

If you decide to rent in Spain, you will find thousands of apartments and villas at prices to suit every pocket.

Some are basically equipped little flats designed for self-catering holidays and often rented by agents in Britain, Holland or Germany. Others are real homes, being let by their owners in the hope of making a little money from their property until they retire to enjoy it full time.

For those coming to Spain to live, it is a good idea to rent a place in the area where they hope to settle permanently so they can make a survey of local conditions before buying. Renting may also be the best plan for people whose capital is in sound investments who do not wish to invest in property.

When you have found a flat or villa that suits your needs, you will be asked to sign a rental contract.

Foreign Contract:

If you are renting a holiday flat for a self-catering visit to Spain, you will probably find this contract in your own language, to be signed in your own country before you leave with the rental company handling the property.

This is perfectly all right. Just make sure the rental company has a sound reputation. Sometimes the accommodation promised you does not measure up to your expectations, so be alert. See below for How to Complain.

The contract forms are usually quite standard, including a list of all the equipment and furnishings, and requiring a deposit to cover any damages the tenant may cause. There is not normally any dispute about the return of this deposit if you have left the flat in good condition.

If you have seen the way some holidaymakers leave their rented flats, you will understand why the companies insist on this deposit.

Spanish Contract:

If you are already in Spain when you rent, you will also be asked to sign a contract. It will specify the amount of the rent, the manner of payment, any deposit and the time period.

Temporada: The contract will be headed, *por temporada,* which means short-term. This is to distinguish it from a long-term rental, called *vivienda,* or residence, because long-term tenants have rights which short-term tenants do not.

A *temporada* contract might even be as long as one year. There is no specific time limit past which a contract becomes long-term.

However, unless otherwise specified in your short-term rental contract, the landlord may put you out at the end of the period stated, or he may offer you a new contract increasing the rent as much as he likes.

These short-term contracts are designed for holiday rentals, not as long-term or permanent residence. Such a *temporada* contract running for one year would be pushing it a little, but the idea is to show the intention of impermanence, so the tenant does not establish full rights. This does not always work as planned. Even short-term tenants can sometimes try to claim a longer contract.

Vivienda: The *vivienda* contract, on the other hand, is meant for those long-term lets when the tenant truly makes the apartment his home. The tenant is much more protected and Spanish law requires that a *vivienda* contract be renewable for a minimum period of five years.

This gives the tenant some stability, as he knows that he has at least this period, and he must be officially notified well in advance of the end of the period if the landlord does not intend to renew the contract.

One-Year Contract
Let's suppose you want to rent a villa in Spain for a year, or even more', and you find that a rental agency in your home country, or even in Spain, has the perfect house at the right price. They offer you a one-year contract, in German or English, with option to renew. This contract, in your own language, will not say that it is either a *temporada* or a *vivienda* contract. The agency does not think in terms of Spanish law, and they don't expect that you will, either.

This foreign-language contract is perfectly legal, although it would have to be translated into Spanish for any court proceedings, and it is a perfectly good offer, which, in fact gives you as the tenant more protection than it gives the landlord.

If you want to renew your contract, you can. If the landlord wants you to leave, you can threaten to go to court, claiming that the villa has become your retirement home. You can say that you will ask the court to have the contract extended to the full five years of the long-term let. Usually the landlord and the agency will be reluctant to become involved in any legal dispute in Spanish courts because they will probably lose their case, and maybe they are not declaring all the rental income for Spanish taxes.

Even if you pay in another country, no matter what the currency, the income derived from property in Spain is still subject to Spanish tax.

No Contract

You may find a charming little flat by the sea, whose owner doesn't want to make any contracts. This can be perfectly all right, too. Just make sure you have clearly written receipts for the rent you pay, which will constitute an implicit contract. Such an implicit rental contract exists even if you don't have the receipts, as soon as the owner cashes your cheque, but it's better to have some piece of paper.

If you are paying month to month in such a situation, the implicit contract ends at the end of each month you pay, or on the date stated on your receipt.

Deposit

The current letting law also establishes the landlord's right to a deposit as a guarantee against damages. The deposit can be held by an agency independent of both landlord and tenant. This agency will not release the deposit until both parties agree.

The deposit consists of one month's rent for a residential unit and two months' rent for commercial premises. The deposit, called a *fianza*, can be held by the housing department of the regional government. In Andalusia, for example, it is deposited with the *Consejería de la Vivienda* of the Andalusian autonomous government, which has offices in major cities.

Registered Contract

For full security in your rental, you want your rental contract registered with the housing department. This means that you will have full legal protection in the event of any court case about your rental.

Let's face it; most rental contracts, especially with foreigners, are simply not registered and the landlords are probably not declaring the rental income for tax purposes. Your contract is still valid in court, but only the registered contract, where the landlord is completely legal in his operations, has the full protection of the law.

It is never a good idea to pay the deposit directly into the landlord's account, as he then is in complete control over whether to release the deposit or not at the end of the let, but it is a common practice.

Tenant Has Right Of First Refusal

In today's fast-moving Spanish real estate market, one of the important rights acquired by a long-term residential tenant is the right of first refusal when the property is put up for sale.

If the landlord sells the property, he is required by law to offer it first to the long-term tenant. He should do this in writing, stating the price and conditions of the sale. If the tenant does not reply or if he refuses the offer, the landlord is then free to sell the property to anyone he chooses under the same conditions.

If the landlord sells the property without informing the tenant in advance, the tenant even has the right to have this sale annulled and to purchase the property himself at the price declared on the sale contract.

As the price of a property sale is often under-declared on Spanish contracts, this means the tenant would buy the property at the lower price which was officially declared. This provision acts as a further deterrent to the landlord.

In Spanish this right is called *tanteo y retracto*.

Tenant May Be Required To Pay Community Fees

Long-term, or *vivienda*, contracts often contain provisions requiring the tenant to pay community fees, that is, the dues charged each year by the property owners' collective for that block of flats, and even the real estate taxes, known as the IBI.

An owner is within his rights to make such a contract, but you should be wary and know what you are getting into. Such extra charges can add up. Furthermore, clauses obliging the tenant to pay the community fees and real estate taxes are considered abusive under Spanish law, and you can protest if you choose, even after you have signed the contract.

If these charges are not mentioned in your contract, they are the owner's responsibility and you can refuse any attempt by him to make you pay for them.

To sum up, in strictly legal terms, the taxes and fees are for the property owner's account. However, it is not illegal for the landlord and tenant to agree in the contract that the tenant will pay them. As long as you know what you are getting into, and the amounts of these charges are clear, and you as the tenant are disposed to accept the price, then it is okay.

If, however, you feel that you have been deceived by the landlord into signing the contract, you can protest the clause and you will surely win your case.

So, we see that the current rental laws aim to provide fair treatment for both landlords and tenants, with safeguards for each party to the contract.

However, we are also going to see that, as soon as a new law is made, someone will try to find a way around it for his own benefit.

Formal Notification Necessary:

Be advised that, if you have a five-year *vivienda* contract and your landlord wishes to terminate your rental at the end of the period, he is obliged to notify you officially, for example, by a notarised letter, well before the end of the period. If he does not notify you officially, the contract can be regarded as renewed for two years and for the same rent.

In any of these situations, most Europeans will find the tenant to have more protection than is normal in many countries. That is, even though the law states that the rental period is finished, a landlord will have some trouble putting out anyone who chooses to stay. He cannot simply summon a policeman and order you out. He must get a court order for this. The procedure will take some time, even when the law is entirely on the landlord's side.

How To Complain:

If you feel that your holiday apartment does not meet the terms of your contract, or if your landlord has abused his side of the deal, you can complain. If you are a genuine tourist, the tourist office of the province or town where the property is located will hear your complaint. If you are a resident, you will do better at the O.M.I.C., the *Oficina Municipal de Información al Consumidor.* This is the consumer information office. Its mission is to deal with consumer problems and these include rents.

Business Premises

More and more foreigners are coming to Spain to start their own businesses. Not the least of their problems is the leasing, purchase or rental of the business premises. This is an area where you really need the best legal advice, apart from your normal good business sense.

LEASING

A Spanish leasehold, which used to be called a *traspaso* but is now known as a *cesión,* gives the lessee the right to re-sell it on to a third party, although he must first offer it to the property owner. If the property owner chooses not to buy back the leasehold at the price asked, the tenant can then sell it to another person, with the landlord having the right to perhaps 10 per cent of the sale.

The new type of leasehold called *cesión* is less rigid than the old *traspaso* and there is no exact legal format required. A property owner and a business tenant can agree on any conditions they choose, which often means that the deal is much more like a normal rental contract. These business rentals or leases are usually open-ended, with no final cut-off point as long as the tenant continues to pay the rent.

When commercial premises are leased, the tenant is now required to withhold Spanish tax of 15 per cent from his rent payments, and pay it to the Spanish tax agency on behalf of the owner.

Watch The Terms
Be particularly alert to the terms of any lease or rental contract you purchase from a presently operating business. Sometimes it is presented by the seller as a leasehold when it is simply a rental agreement which gives the tenant no rights to any of the profit from re-selling it.

When you are asked to pay a large sum of money for a "leasehold", you want to be very sure that you are buying something which you will later have the right to sell. If all that is being offered is a rental agreement, then you are paying for nothing.

This has happened to more than one business purchaser in Spain, who sees the term *traspaso* on the contract heading and believes he is buying a lease, when the contract, when carefully read, turns out to be just a rental.

Take legal advice before you get into a Spanish lease.

GLOSSARY

Alquiler – Rental

Arrendamiento – Rental, lease

Cesión – Lease

Contrato de Vivienda – Long-term residential contract

Contrato por Temporada – Short-term holiday contract

Fianza – Deposit

Inquilino – tenant

Ley de Arrendamiento Urbano – Rental law

Propietario – Owner, landlord

Tanteo y Retracto – Right of first refusal to buy property

Traspaso – Old form of leasehold

5.   TAXES ON PROPERTY

PART ONE -
CAPITAL GAINS TAX ON SALE PROFITS

Anyone who buys property in Spain today will be liable to pay Spanish capital gains tax when he sells his flat or villa in the future.

This applies to residents and non-residents alike.

Residents pay a maximum of 15 per cent and their capital gains are calculated as part of their Spanish income tax.

Non-residents pay a flat rate of 35 per cent. Buyers from non-resident sellers are required to withhold five per cent of the total purchase price and pay it directly to the Spanish Tax Agency, thus making sure that the seller does not take the money and run.

Until December 31, 1996, both residents and non-residents could deduct 11.11 per cent per year from their profits, after the first two years of ownership, and pay no tax at all after 10 years. This favourable picture has ended.

There are four special situations in which a property seller is not liable for capital gains tax. Let's see if you are among the lucky ones.

1. Residents Over 65 Exempt
An official resident of Spain 65 years of age and over, who has held a residence permit for three years and lived in his principal residence for three years, is not subject to capital gains tax when he sells the residence.

If you are 65 or over and hold a Spanish residence permit, you can buy a principal residence this year and sell it in three years for a fat profit in today's brisk real estate market, and have no capital gains tax to pay.

2. Residents Get Rollover Credit For New Home
An official resident of Spain who reinvests all of the proceeds of his house sale to purchase another Spanish home as his principal residence will get complete relief from this tax. He must have lived in the home for three years to qualify. If he uses only a portion of the total amount of his house sale, he will get a percentage of relief up to the amount reinvested.

One typical situation is where an older couple sell their large villa, which they no longer need, and move into a smaller apartment, using the rest of their profits to improve their life style. If we suppose that the couple originally bought the villa for   200,000 and sell it today for   260,000, they have a profit of   60,000.

If they buy a new flat for the whole of the   260,000 selling price, they will have no Spanish capital gains tax to pay. But if they buy a small flat for   130,000, and keep the remaining   130,000 in cash, they will have used only one-half of their sale proceeds to purchase a new principal residence.

Thus, they get to deduct only one-half of their profits.

Half of 60,000 is 30,000 free of tax, but they must pay tax on the other half. As residents, their maximum capital gains tax is 15 per cent, so they will pay 4,500.

3. Buyers Before December 31, 1986

If you bought your Spanish property before December 31, 1986, you are free of capital gains tax. This applies to both residents and non-residents.

As we noted above, under the previous capital gains regulations, those who owned their property for 10 years were free of tax. This provision ended in 1996, making 1986 the final cut-off date for exemption.

4. Holders of Usufruct

A recent change in capital gains regulations exempts elderly persons who use the "inherit from yourself" schemes in which you sell your house but retain the right to live in it until your death.

A person 65 or older who contracts with a company to sell his principal residence in exchange for the lifetime right to inhabit the dwelling, along with a monthly payment, will not be taxed on any capital gain involved. This makes such deals to turn your home ownership into lifetime income more attractive for older persons of modest means. The right to inhabit the property is called a *usufructo*.

If you do not fall into one of these groups, you will be liable for capital gains tax when you sell your property.

We can distinguish three possible situations for sellers of Spanish property today. These are:

1. Long-term Owners: The fortunate long-term owners who bought their homes before December 31, 1986, meaning they have owned them for 10 years before December 31, 1996. They have no Spanish capital gains tax to pay when they sell now. If they are non-residents, they are not subject to the five per cent retention.

Transitional Sellers: Those who bought in the period from 1987 through 1994. They have the right to the 11.11 per cent per year reduction, starting after the first two years of ownership, but only up to 1996. Those who bought in 1995 have no reduction because their initial two-year period of no reduction runs up against the December 31, 1996, cut-off point. These sellers can also apply the inflation correction factor (see below).

3. Today's Buyers: Those who purchase today (and really, since 1995) will have no 11.11 per cent reductions at all. Their only help is the application of a coefficient that corrects for inflation. Nevertheless, it is a help because it is applied to the entire amount of your original purchase price, rather than to the amount of your profit, so you don't pay much more tax than under the old system.

If you sell your Spanish property today, you will fall into one of these categories. Let's take them one by one.

Long-Term Owners

If you are one of the fortunate long-term owners who bought before December 31, 1986, you have no tax to pay, so you may skip this section.

If you are a "transitional seller" in Group 2, you have the most complicated calculation. Here is an example.

Step by Step For Transitional Sellers

1. Find the price you paid for your property originally. This will be the price entered on your *escritura*. If you did as many other Spanish buyers did a few years ago and entered a price lower than the price you actually paid, you will suffer for it now. Let's suppose you bought in 1990 and your registered price is 15 million pesetas.

2. Convert this price into euros. It comes to just over 90,000.

3. Now add onto your price all the official expenses you had in acquiring the property. After your purchase was complete, you should have attached the receipts for the taxes, fees and other expenses to your title deed for your files. Add to your original purchase price the amount of property transfer tax you paid at the time, at 6 per cent, or at 7.5 per cent if you bought a new property from a developer, thus paying IVA instead of transfer tax. Enter expenses for notary, property registration, the *plus valía* tax if you as the buyer had to pay it, and lawyer. You need the official receipts for these payments in order to claim them.

4. Convert these peseta expenses into euros at 166 pesetas to the euro.

5. Let's suppose that these expenses total just over 10 per cent of your price, or 10,000. You add them in, making a total acquisition cost of 100,000.

6. Apply inflation corrector. Your purchase was in 1990 and the money has become worth less today because of inflation. You can apply the inflation correction factor from the table below to bring that 100,000 to today's values. Looking at the table we see that any purchase before 1994 has a factor of 1.1690. Multiply this by 100,000 and you get 116.900. Those of you who are mathematically minded will notice that this does not really correct for all the inflation since 1990. However, the tax agency knows that you transitional sellers will also have the reduction factor of 11.11 per cent per year to apply. I told you it was complicated.

7. In order to apply your reductions, you have to calculate your

profit. You are selling today for   330,000, triplng your money in 14 years. Not too bad. And you are declaring the full amount on the contract. Subtract selling expenses from your total. You can reduce your total selling price by any justified expenses. If you have a bill from your estate agent, with IVA, you can deduct this. If the commission is five per cent, let's call that a nice round   10,000.

Calculate your profit. If your total acquisition cost, corrected for inflation, is   101,600 and your reduced selling price, as declared, is   210,000, this makes your profit on paper   108,400.

8. Now you get to apply the reduction percentage to this profit. If you bought in 1990, your factor starts in 1992, after your first two years of ownership. The factor ends in 1996, so you get four years´ worth. Four times 11.11 per cent is, rounding off, 44 per cent. Apply this to   200,000 and let's say you have   88,000 worth of reduction. Subtract this from   200,000 and you have a corrected and taxable profit of   112,000

So far, this operation applies to residents and non-residents alike, but now we see a difference in their taxation.

RESIDENT PAYS AS INCOME TAX

A resident pays his capital gains tax as part of his income tax. If you sell in 2005, you do not declare this until May of 2006, when you file for Spanish income tax.

In Spanish, capital gain is called *incremento de patrimonio,* and there is a section of the tax form especially designed for it.

The resident pays his capital gains tax at exactly the same rate as he pays his Spanish income tax. If you are of modest income, paying Spanish income tax somewhere around 15 per cent, you will also pay your capital gains tax at 15 per cent.

In the present case, 15 per cent of   112,000 is   16,800 tax you will pay on a profit of more than   200,000, having owned the property for 15 years.

Even if your income is very high, the absolute limit on capital gains tax for a resident is 15 per cent. This means that you could never pay more than   15,000 on a profit of   100,000.

NON-RESIDENT PAYS 35 PER CENT

The non-resident, however, faces a tax of 35 per cent. In our example, this gives a tax of   39,000, more than twice the resident's tax.

If the non-resident is tempted to take the money and run, remember that the buyer does not pay him the full price. He must withhold five per cent of the total purchase price and pay it directly to the Spanish Tax Agency, filing form 211. The Notary demands to see the paid-up form 211 at the signing of the deeds, so there is no escape.

In the example, five per cent of   330,000 is   16,500. The seller still owes another   28,500 on top of this. He is required to file Form 212 within 30 days and pay the rest of his tax. If he decides to become a tax dodger, he can leave Spain, owing the Tax Agency   28,500, not a big profit for the risk.

If the deposit of five per cent turns out to be greater than the amount of tax owed by the non-resident, he can also claim a refund on the same Form 212, which should be filed within 30 days of the transaction.

The Tax Agency promises to return the over-payment within 90 days, but many report that they take as long as a year.

TODAY'S SELLERS

Well, we told you it was complicated. If you fall into the third category of seller, those who bought after 1994, you have only the inflation correction factor to apply.

Coeficiente de Actualización
Inflation Correction Table

PURCHASE DATE	2005 SALE
1994 and earlier	1.1690
1995	1.2350
1996	1.1928
1997	1.1690
1998	1.1463
1999	1.1257
2000	1.1040
2001	1.0824
2002	1.0612
2003	1.0404
2004	1.0200
2005	1.0000

That is, if you bought in 1996 and you sell today for 200,000, you look at the table and see that the factor is 1.1928. After you have added in all your acquisition costs, let's suppose that your total cost in 1996 is a nice round 100,000.

Apply the factor and you get 119,280. This reduces your taxable profit from 100,000 to 80,000 and saves you about 7,000 in capital gains tax if you are a non-resident. It doesn't look like a great savings, but it's better than nothing.

SECTION TWO - TAXES YOU PAY EVERY YEAR

All property owners in Spain are liable for three separate taxes every year. These taxes are:
1. Property Owners' Imputed Income Tax
2. Wealth Tax
3. Annual Real Estate Tax

Property Owners' Imputed Income Tax

The good news for residents is that Spain's property owners' imputed income tax is no longer payable on the owner's principal residence.

A non-resident must continue to pay the yearly tax, however, because he is not resident in Spain, so his principal dwelling cannot be here. Residents who own more than one dwelling will also continue to be subject to the tax on their second home or other property.

Persons subject to this tax have two per cent of the *valor catastral*, the official rated value, of their property attributed to them as a sort of imaginary income. This figure is 1.1 per cent if your rated value has been raised sharply since 1994, and most values have been raised.

Residents pay their tax on this notional income by having it added to their other income as if it were more earnings. This means that they pay tax at their normal income tax rate. If their incomes are modest they will pay 15 per cent and if their incomes are high they will pay 30 or even 40 per cent.

The non-resident is taxed always at the flat rate of 25 per cent on any income arising in Spain. Do not confuse this tax of 25 per cent on earnings with the capital gains tax of 35 per cent, which applies to profits from the sale of assets, such as a house or shares in a company.

If a non-resident husband and wife own a villa which has a *valor catastral* of 120,000 but a higher real value of 180,000, we find that the Spanish Tax Agency imputes to them separately an ownership of

60,000 each, half of the *valor catastral*.

We then calculate that 2 per cent of 60,000 is 1,200 of imaginary income. Taxed at 25 per cent, this gives a bill of 300 for each of the two owners, total 600 annually on the property.

"Wealth Tax"

In addition to his income tax the Spanish resident – and non-resident property owner – is liable for Spain's tax on capital assets – *patrimonio* tax. The name "wealth tax" may not sound like proper legal terminology, but it is an adequate translation of the Spanish name, as it's exactly that: a tax on all your assets and property; your total wealth.

In Spanish, the name is *impuesto extraordinario sobre el patrimonio*, the extraordinary tax on assets. This tax started in 1978 as a special measure to force many Spanish citizens who had been hiding their wealth, especially property, to bring these assets into the open.

Hacienda placed a very small tax on these assets, amounting to only .002, that is two-tenths of one per cent, or two-thousandths of the taxable base, up to assets of 167,129. After that, the rate goes up as assets go up. Wealth tax is based on the real sale value declared in the contract, which is almost always higher than the *valor catastral*. In most cases, an owner can legally declare a value of two times the *valor catastral*, or even less. This is because the Tax Agency knows that real values can fluctuate with the property market. The multiplier of the rateable value varies from town to town, and may be even less than two times.

PATRIMONIO TAX RATES 2005
(Rounded to nearest euro)

Taxable Base	Tax	Rate Band	Marginal rate %
0	0	167,129	0.20
167,129	334	167,123	0.30
334,253	836	334,247	0.50
716,581	2,507	668,500	0.90
1,337,000	8,523	1,337,000	1.30
2,673,999	25,904	2,673,999	1.70
5,347,998	71,362	5,347998	2.10
10,695,996	183,670	excess	2.50

You declare for this tax when you declare for your income tax, on the simplified Form 214 if you are a non-resident with only one property, or on the separate wealth tax Form 714.

Wealth tax affects residents and non-residents differently. A resident is required to declare his world-wide assets while the non-resident declares only his property and assets in Spain.

These taxable assets can include bank deposits, stocks, shares, bonds, ownership of a business, gold bars under the mattress, automobiles, yachts, private airplanes, works of art unless they are owned by the maker, jewels, luxury fur coats or anything else that can be considered wealth. Your home furnishings are exempt unless they are valuable antiques. There are deductions available for debts against your business, mortgages on your property, and any tax of a similar nature paid in a foreign country.

The principal deduction for a resident of Spain is that he pays nothing on the first   108,182. A husband and wife each have an exemption of   108,182, and each must make an individual declaration. Further, if the asset in question is a principal residence, each person has an exemption of   150,253 on top of the   108,182.

If a husband and wife own together a property valued at almost   300,000, they each declare half the value, take their exemption of more than   300,000, and have no *patrimonio* tax to pay.

As Spanish law views property as individually owned, for wealth tax purposes, this means that a husband and wife who own their home together, must each file a wealth tax declaration declaring 50 per cent of the value as their property.

Non-Resident Pays On Form 214

None of the exemptions above apply to non-residents. They must pay from the first euro of valuation. The non-resident, however, is taxed only on his assets located in Spain.

Non-residents declare on their own special tax Form 214 every year. (see forms at end of chapter).

In our example above for non-resident property tax, the estimated market value of the property is   180,000. This is in fact less than two times their valor catastral of 120,000, so our couple legally declares this value of   180,000. Two-tenths of one per cent of this is   360, or   180 for each of the husband and wife half-owners.

Add to that   600 of Spanish non-resident property owner imputed income tax, divided into   300 each, and you get a total of   480 due to the Spanish tax man from each of the co-owning spouses, or   960 total from both spouses. This is in addition to your annual real estate tax. (see below)

If we imagine that your annual real estate tax, IBI, on the villa is 240, this means that it will cost you   1,200 a year in Spanish taxes simply to own the place.

Non-residents using Form 214 can declare at any time during the year.

Keep in mind that, if you own two properties in Spain, you cannot use Form 214 and must declare on Form 714 for wealth tax and Form 210 for imputed income tax, and you must declare in the period between May 1 and June 20.

If you own two properties, you are still required to name an official *representante fiscal*, a tax representative in Spain (see details in section Your Fiscal Representative).

One owner who applied for Form 214 was annoyed to discover that he was not eligible because he had purchased his garage separately from his house. Because he has two separate title deeds, he must fill out the standard forms, declare in the regular time period and name an official tax representative.

In addition to this, both residents and non-residents pay the annual real estate tax.

ANNUAL REAL ESTATE TAX (IBI)

The annual real estate tax on your Spanish property must also be paid. This tax, based on your *valor catastral*, can vary widely from town to town for the same type of property because it is a municipal tax. You can expect to pay much more for a townhouse in Marbella than you would pay for the same accommodation in an inland provincial town. If you live in a typical village house set back from the coast, your annual real estate tax could be as little as   100. If you have a well-positioned villa on a large lot you could pay as much as   3,000.

This real estate tax is called the IBI, the *Impuesto sobre Bienes Inmuebles*. The tax is raised every year, as a result of inflation.

If you are a non-resident, the best solution for you is to have the tax *domiciliado* in your bank. This is a standing order to the bank to pay the tax — and you can include any other municipal charges as well. You obtain a form at the bank which authorises them to pay the tax bill, and you deposit a copy of the form with your *ayuntamiento*. This tells them where to send the bill. You are thus assured that your taxes are paid when they are due, the same as the telephone, water and electric bills.

If you prefer to pay the bill in person, you will have to go to your town hall and pay it each year. Some towns offer a discount for early payment, so be sure to ask.

In addition to the *valor catastral*, the assessed value of your property for tax purposes, the IBI also lists your *referencia catastral* number, which will locate your property at the *Catastro* office, along with its officially measured dimensions. This can be important in buying and selling property because sometimes the physical description does not agree with the description given in the property title.

If you think that you can simply forget about these three taxes because you are not a Spanish resident and someday will sell your home in the sun anyway, think again.

The Spanish tax agency, Hacienda, will check the books at the time of the property sale. They will be holding that deposit of 5 per cent of your total sale price, remember. It is a guarantee against the owners imputed income tax and wealth tax obligations for the last four years, as well as against the capital gains liability. You will also be required to present the current real estate tax receipt, the IBI, when you sign the sale contract.

COMMUNITY CHARGES

The fees charged annually by your Community of Property Owners, to pay for your share of maintaining the community property, are not taxes of course, but they need to be factored into your totals when you are calculating the annual running costs of your Spanish property. These fees might be as little as   400 a year for a small flat or more like   4,000 a year for a luxury villa on an elegant estate in Marbella.

RENTAL OR BUSINESS INCOME - FORM 210

All non-residents who are making money by renting out their Spanish property are subject to tax on this income arising in Spain. They are required to declare their Spanish income on Form 210. They are supposed to declare within 30 days of receiving the income, but they can apply to make their declarations quarterly to save paperwork.

Such non-resident income is taxed at the flat rate of 25 per cent.

If you are a non-resident but you own and operate a business in Spain, such as a restaurant, or a bar, or a cement factory, you are also liable for Spanish tax on your profits.

97

YOUR FISCAL REPRESENTATIVE

The non-resident property owner of only one property is no longer required by Spanish law to name a fiscal representative who is resident in Spain. Those who own two or more properties must do so, however, under penalty of fines that can go as high as 6,000 if he does not comply.

The fiscal representative assures the Spanish tax authorities that they have a reliable contact inside Spain for the non-resident taxpayer. Although most non-residents name their tax consultant or lawyer as their fiscal representative, it can be anyone, even a foreigner, as long as he is officially resident in Spain. Any *gestoría* or tax office has the simple forms necessary.

NON-RESIDENT'S FISCAL IDENTIFICATION NUMBER

If you are a non-resident property owner, you will have the above-mentioned taxes to pay and perhaps a fiscal representative to name. In order to pay these taxes, you must apply for a *Número de Identificación de Extranjero,* a NIE, which is your Spanish tax identification number. Residents, of course, have a number as well, and Spaniards do, too.

In fact, you should apply for this number when you purchase your property. The number identifies you to the Spanish taxman and is required when you pay your taxes or have any dealings with the Tax Agency.

To obtain it, present yourself at the nearest police *comisaría* with a foreigners' department, along with a photocopy of the first pages of your passport. Fill in the form and wait a few weeks for your number to be assigned. You can also have your *gestoría* do this for you.

Then you will be registered with Hacienda's central computers just like the rest of us in today's electronically observed society.

SPECIAL TAX ON OFFSHORE COMPANIES

During the property boom of the 1980s thousands of luxury homes on the Spanish Costas were sold on the basis of ownership through a non-resident company. Many of these offshore companies are located in the so-called "tax havens" where little or no local taxes are charged and the names of the owners are confidential.

On the Costa del Sol, entire urbanisations were marketed with

Gibraltar companies already formed to own the property. The buyer purchased the Gibraltar company, in Gibraltar, and his real name never appeared on any Spanish documents, only the name of the Gibraltar company.

Estimates are that at least 12,000 companies exist, in Gibraltar alone, without mentioning other offshore tax havens, for the sole purpose of owning property in Spain. These companies were created, quite legally, as a means to slide around a number of Spanish taxes while concealing the identity of the true owners of the property.

Other non-resident companies are located in European countries where they are subject to tax like any other company, including tax on their assets in Spain.

There is nothing incorrect about this sort of operation, and it means that all Spanish transfer taxes – which can amount to 10 per cent of the price – are bypassed when property owned by such companies changes hands. This is because only the offshore company is bought and sold, a transaction which takes place outside of Spain. As far as the Spanish government is concerned, the property is still owned by the same company, and no change has taken place, so no tax is due. This offshore company ownership also avoids Spanish inheritance tax. The company is not registered in Spain, even though it possesses an asset here, so no Spanish inheritance tax is charged when the company is bequeathed to its inheritor, who then continues to own the company through Gibraltar, the Channel Islands, or some other country.

This is all perfectly legal. Nevertheless, it is not quite cricket and finally the loss of tax revenue irritated the Spanish authorities so much that they enacted a special tax on offshore companies. They are not the first to do so. In fact they were just about the last country in Europe to permit these operations.

SPECIAL TAX IS 3 PER CENT

This special tax on offshore companies is 3 per cent of the *valor catastral*. This means that, if your property is valued at 100,000 (with a real market value of perhaps 200,000), your annual tax is 3,000.

For companies registered in Gibraltar or other tax havens around the world, there are absolutely no exemptions. Spain's tax ministry has a list of jurisdictions regarded as "tax havens".

When both the company and its real owners are fiscal residents of "normal" countries which have taxation treaties with Spain, the company can claim exemption from the tax of 3 per cent. They must reveal all details of the owners, and present certification that the company pays its taxes in its country of registration.

The law is designed to crack down on those persons taking advantage of secrecy provisions in tax havens while permitting normal EU companies to continue to own property in Spain as long as they pay their taxes at home.

This leaves perfectly legitimate owners of tax haven companies, however, in the position of either having to pay the stiff tax or divest themselves of their companies.

If they "sell" the property to themselves as the new individual owners, this operation attracts tax at about 10 per cent of the total operation, just like any normal property sale. Some lawyers have been able to wind up the Gibraltar company and distribute its assets to the owners, under a small business tax of one per cent, plus a few other charges that bring the total expense to about three per cent.

This leaves you as an individual owning your home in Spain, just like almost everyone else, and subject to all the usual Spanish taxes we have discussed.

As the tax is based on the *valor catastral*, the assessed value, paying the tax might be a viable option in situations where this value is much lower than the real value. There are still cases where properties that are worth 200,000 on the market have an assessed value of 50,000, for example.

In such cases and where the individual has special need for confidentiality in his ownership, it could be a possible course of action. Be warned, however, that Spain continues its process of raising the *valor catastral* towards normal market prices. Furthermore, European Union commissions are now exerting stricter controls over tax havens as part of the EU campaign to discover the hiding places of black money obtained through various types of illegal operations.

Each case will need individual study and some careful planning.

GLOSSARY

Ayuntamiento – Town hall, where you pay IBI

Coeficiente de Actualización – Inflation correction factor

Contribuyente – Taxpayer

Formulario – Form, as in taxes

Impuesto – Tax

IBI Impuesto sobre Bienes Inmuebles – Annual real estate tax

Impuesto sobre el Patrimonio – Capital assets or wealth tax

Incremento de Patrimonio – Capital gain

Modelo – Form, as in taxes

NIE (Numero de Identificación de Extranjero) – Foreigner's tax identification number.

Paraíso Fiscal – Tax haven

Patrimonio – Capital assets, wealth

Referencia Catastral – Reference number for property inscription in the Castastro Registry

Representante Fiscal – Official tax representative of foreigner

Valor Catastral – Rated value of property for tax purposes

Usufructo – Usufruct, right to inhabit property

FORM 211

This is the form used for declaring your deposit of five per cent paid to Spain's Tax Agency when you purchase property from a non-resident.

Datos del Adquirente: Here you enter name, address and details of the buyer, including his NIE, his tax identification number in Spain, even though Form says NIF. If you have Hacienda stickers, *etiquetas,* you can use these instead.

Devengo: Date of the sale.

Datos del Transmitente: Enter details of the non-resident seller. Where it says: "Clave País", a separate sheet gives you a three-digit number code for every country.

Representante: If you have a fiscal representative in Spain (not required if you own only one property) you enter his details here.

Descripción del Inmueble: Description of the property, including the address, whether or not it is being transmitted through a private document or a public document signed before a Notary, and, if so, the Notary and his registration number of the contract. Finally, enter the Catastral Reference number, found on the IBI receipt.

Liquidación: The liquidation is the calculation of the amount. Here you enter the declared price of the sale and calculate five per cent of it.

Adquirente: Buyer signs, with date.

Ingreso: Enter your form of payment, whether in cash or by certified cheque made out to "Tesoro Público".

Agencia Tributaria

Delegación de

Administración de   Código

Impuesto sobre la Renta de no Residentes

DECLARACIÓN-DOCUMENTO DE INGRESO

Modelo
211
RETENCIÓN EN LA ADQUISICIÓN DE BIENES INMUEBLES A NO RESIDENTES SIN ESTABLECIMIENTO PERMANENTE

211000008507 6

Datos del adquirente

Espacio reservado para la etiqueta identificativa

Devengo

Fecha de devengo ....

N.I.F.   F/J   APELLIDOS Y NOMBRE (por este orden) o RAZÓN SOCIAL   N.º adquirentes

Calle/Plaza/Avda: Número   Esc.   Piso   Prta.   Teléfono

Código Postal   Municipio   Provincia/País   Clave País

Datos del transmitente no residente

N.I.F.   F/J   APELLIDOS Y NOMBRE (por este orden) o RAZÓN SOCIAL   N.º transmitentes

Dirección Postal

Municipio   País   Clave País

Datos del representante

N.I.F.   F/J   APELLIDOS Y NOMBRE (por este orden) o RAZÓN SOCIAL

Calle/Plaza/Avda.   Número   Esc.   Piso   Prta.   Teléfono

Código Postal   Municipio   Provincia

Descripción del inmueble

Calle/Plaza/Avda.   Número   Esc.   Piso   Prta.

Código Postal   Municipio   Provincia

Doc. público   Doc. privado   Notario o fedatario   N.º de protocolo

Referencia catastral

Liquidación

Importe de la transmisión 01

Total a ingresar (5% de 01) 02

Adquirente

Fecha:

Firma:

Ingreso

TESORO PÚBLICO, Cuenta restringida de Caja de la Delegación o Administración de la A.E.A.T.

Forma de pago: ☐ Dinero de curso legal   ☐ Cheque conformado y nominativo a favor del Tesoro Público

Importe: I

Espacio reservado para la Administración

Ejemplar para la Administración

103

FORM 212

This is the form on which the non-resident declares his capital gain or loss when he sells his Spanish property. On this form the non-resident seller either applies for a refund, if the deposit of 5 per cent is greater than the tax, or makes an extra payment, if the deposit is less than the tax due.

Contribuyente: List your name and address and fiscal number, or, if you have them, affix one of your tax labels here. F/J is "F" for a person and "J" for a company. If spouses declare together, give percentage of ownership. "Código Extranjero" is for your tax number in your home country.

Cónyuge: Fiscal number and name and percentage of ownership of the spouse.

Representante: If you have a Fiscal Representative in Spain, enter his details here.

Adquirente: List details of the buyer.

Descripción: Description of the property. Give the name of the Notary before whom the contract was signed and list his Protocol Number for it.

Liquidación: Liquidation is the calculation of the tax on your capital gain. First, list the number of the Form 211 on which your buyer registered his five per cent deposit. Enter in Box 1 the net price you received after deducting all your expenses involved in the sale. In Box 2 enter your original cost of acquiring the property, adding in all your expenses at the time, such as taxes and legal fees. You apply the inflation correction factor at this point. See the text for examples of calculations. In Box 3 you enter the difference. If you bought your property before Dec. 31, 1994, you now apply the 11.11 per cent per year factor, as described in the text, in order to get your tax base, entered in Box 4. The second table is for any additions made to the property. Box 4 will then be your taxable base, entered again in Box 9. Your tax rate will be 35 per cent as a non-resident.

Enter total tax in Box 11. Subtract 5 per cent, shown in Box 13, and you have the "Cuota Diferencial", the amount you must either pay or claim back on the second sheet of Form 212 (Not shown).

Modelo 212 — Impuesto sobre la Renta de no Residentes. No residentes sin establecimiento permanente.

212000009816 0

Ejemplar para la Administración

FORM 213

This is the form on which you either declare and pay your annual tax of 3 per cent on the *valor catastral*, or rated value, of your Spanish property owned by a non-resident company, or on which you cite your non-resident company's exemption from the tax.

Entidad Sujeta: Either paste in your Tax Agency label, or fill in the details of the non-resident company. "Código Extranjero" is the tax number, if it has one, in the country of registration.

Devengo: Enter year for which tax is being paid.

Representante: If the company has a fiscal representative in Spain, enter his details here.

Exenciones: Companies which are exempt from the tax check the appropriate box here. If your company is not located in a tax haven, and it pays its taxes in a "normal" country, check Box 1, and so on. Only those non-resident companies located in tax havens must pay.

Liquidación: Your "Base Imponible" is the *valor catastral* of the property. Tax rate is 3 per cent of that value. If you have owned the property less than a full year, you will have a proportional reduction. Otherwise you pay the full tax. When a company has several owners, some of whom are entitled to exemption and others not, there is a reduction as well.

NOTE: FORM 213 has two other sheets, one of them for listing all properties owned by the company, and another for entering the details of persons owning the company when exemption is requested because the company pays its taxes in a normal jurisdiction and discloses the names of its real owners.

MINISTERIO DE ECONOMÍA Y HACIENDA

Agencia Tributaria

Delegación de

Administración de — Código

Impuesto sobre la Renta de no Residentes

Gravamen Especial sobre Bienes Inmuebles de Entidades no Residentes

DECLARACIÓN-LIQUIDACIÓN/DOCUMENTO DE INGRESO

Modelo **213**

GRAVAMEN ESPECIAL SOBRE BIENES INMUEBLES DE ENTIDADES NO RESIDENTES

213000001935 0

Entidad sujeta al gravamen

Espacio reservado para la etiqueta identificativa

(Si no dispone de etiquetas, haga constar a continuación sus datos identificativos, así como los de su domicilio fiscal)

Devengo

Ejercicio ....

N.I.F. — Razón social de la entidad

Calle/Plaza/Avda. — Número — Esc. — Piso — Prta. — Teléfono

Código Postal — Municipio — Provincia

Domicilio de la entidad en el país de residencia — Código extranjero

Residencia fiscal: país — Código país — Nacionalidad

Representante

N.I.F. — Apellidos y Nombre o Razón social

Calle/Plaza/Avda. — Número — Esc. — Piso — Prta. — Teléfono

Código Postal — Municipio — Provincia — Fecha otorgamiento poder

Exenciones

Entidades exentas (artículo 32.5 de la Ley 41/1998, del Impuesto sobre la Renta de no Residentes):

1) Entidades con derecho a la aplicación de un Convenio para evitar la doble imposición que contenga cláusula de intercambio de información, en los términos y con los requisitos del artículo 32.5.b) de la Ley 41/1998.

2) Entidades que desarrollan en España, de modo continuado o habitual, explotaciones económicas diferenciables de la simple tenencia o arrendamiento de los inmuebles en los términos del artículo 7.2 del Reglamento del Impuesto sobre la Renta de no Residentes. Epígrafe del Impuesto sobre Actividades Económicas.

3) Sociedades que coticen en mercados secundarios de valores oficialmente reconocidos.

4) Entidades sin ánimo de lucro de carácter benéfico o cultural, en los términos del artículo 32.5.e) de la Ley 41/1998.

Liquidación

Base imponible 01

Cuota (3% de 01) 02

Porcentaje de reducción .... 03 %

Reducción en la cuota 04

Cuota a ingresar 02 - 04 05

Negativas

CUOTA CERO

Declarante

Fecha:

Firma:

Ingreso

TESORO PÚBLICO. Cuenta restringida de Caja de la Delegación o Administración de la A.E.A.T.

Forma de pago: Dinero de curso legal — Cheque conformado y nominativo a favor del Tesoro Público

Importe: I

Este documento no será válido sin la certificación mecánica o, en su defecto, firma autorizada

Ejemplar para la Administración

FORM 214

This form is used by non-resident property owners to declare their Spanish capital assets tax, the *patrimonio,* also called wealth tax, and their non-resident property owner's imputed income tax, on the same one-page form. Residents are not subject to this tax on their principal dwelling.

Contribuyente: Stick on your Tax Agency printed label, or fill in the form with your name and address. Put your NIE where it says NIF.

Devengo: Enter the year.

Liquidación Patrimonio: For *patrimonio* tax, you enter the real declared price of the property in Box 1. (See Tax chapter for values you may declare). Enter any debts against it, such as mortgages, in Box 2. The difference is your taxable base, Box 3. The percentages of the tax are given in a table on the back of the form and also in this book.

Liquidación Renta: To get Box 5, you apply to the *valor catastral* of the property either 2 per cent, or 1.1 per cent if your property has been sharply valued upward since 1994. Box 5 is your imaginary income. To this you apply 25 per cent, the non-resident income tax, to get Box 6, the amount of the tax.

Total: Add your two taxes together.

Vivienda: Enter details of the property, including the catastral reference number from your IBI receipt.

Representante: If you have a fiscal representative, list him here.

Declarante: Sign your name, with the date.

Ingreso: Enter your form of payment, cash or certified cheque.

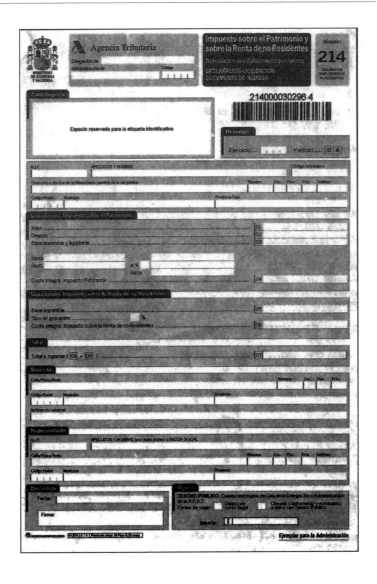

6. SPANISH WILLS AND INHERITANCE TAX

SPANISH WILLS AND INHERITANCE TAX

Once you own property in Spain, you should think about making a Spanish will and about paying Spanish inheritance tax. You should give this some thought even before you purchase because you may want to put the property in the name of your heirs right now, retaining the lifetime right to live in it for yourself. (See last section).

There are four main points to bear in mind in connection with Spanish wills:

1. You should make a Spanish will disposing of your Spanish property in order to avoid time-consuming and expensive legal problems for your heirs. Make a separate will disposing of assets located outside of Spain.

2. As a foreigner, you will probably find that Spanish authorities do not oblige you to follow the Spanish law of compulsory heirs, in which you must leave two-thirds of your estate to your children. You can leave your estate to whomever you choose, as long as your own national law permits this. Your estate, however, will be subject to Spanish inheritance tax, which can be high when property is left to non-relatives.

3. There are very few ways around Spanish inheritance taxes and these legal ways require careful advance planning. Spanish law provides no large exemption from inheritance tax, such as most countries have when the family home is transferred. The tax is due after the first 16,000, even on the family home.

4. However, if you are an official resident of Spain leaving your property to a spouse or child who is also a resident, you may be eligible for a 95 per cent reduction in the value of the property for inheritance tax calculation up to a limit of 120,000. In the region of Andalusia there is a further reduction for estates under 500,000, again for resident owners. These reductions are not available to non-residents.

Let's look at these points in more detail.

Spanish Inheritance Laws Restrict Freedom

In order to protect the family and provide for the children, Spanish inheritance laws, like Scottish laws, restrict the testator's freedom to leave his property to anyone he pleases.

It is almost impossible for a Spanish parent to make the classic threat that he will cut the no-good son out of his will. This is because Spanish law requires a parent to leave two-thirds of his estate to his children, even by-passing the surviving spouse. In general, most people wish to provide for their children, so they have no problem in making a Spanish will in accordance with those provisions.

But let us first establish just what the estate consists of when a person dies.

In Spanish law, a surviving spouse keeps all assets acquired before the marriage, half of the goods acquired during marriage, and all personal gifts or inheritances which have come directly to this spouse.

Assuming that most of the couple's assets were acquired during their marriage, this means that about half of their assets do not really form part of the deceased person's estate. Half of the property continues to belong to the surviving spouse.

This is particularly true of real estate. If the names of husband and wife both figure on the title deed of the property, each has one half of the ownership. Thus, when one dies, only half of the Spanish property is transmitted. The living spouse continues to own his or her half, with his or her name on the title deed.

CHILDREN ARE COMPULSORY HEIRS

Of the rest of the assets, only one-third can be freely disposed of, under the Spanish law of *herederos forzosos,* or obligatory heirs.

When a person dies leaving children, the estate is divided into three equal parts.

One of these thirds must be left to surviving issue in equal parts. Another third must also be left to the children, but the testator may decide how to divide it. That is, he can choose to leave all of this third to only one of his children or grandchildren. A surviving spouse has a life interest in this third. If the estate is a house or a piece of property, the child who inherits it cannot dispose of it freely until his surviving parent dies, because the surviving parent holds an usufruct over the property.

The final third of the estate can be freely willed to anyone the testator chooses.

NOTE: The administration of inheritances has passed from the central government in Madrid to the various autonomous regions of Spain. Some of these regions have different provisions in their laws. If you live in Aragon, for example, it is half of the estate which must go to children, not two-thirds. Check locally for details.

If a foreign resident dies in Spain without a will, his estate in Spain will be distributed according to the Spanish laws of succession.

Example: Suppose that a husband and father dies, leaving a widow and three children. The only property is the house. The widow continues to own half the house, because her name is on the title deed as half-owner. The other half of the house constitutes the estate.

This is divided equally among the three children. When the estate is settled, each child will have one-third title to half of the house, meaning that each one now owns one-sixth of the house, and the title deed has four names on it, the widow and each of the three children. The widow also holds an usufruct — *usufructo* — on the children's share. This means she can use their half of the property until she dies, as well as her own half. They must all agree and sign the deed if the house is to be sold.

It is this provision of the inheritance law that causes the situation frequently seen in the Spanish countryside and villages, where six brothers are part-owners of a finca or a pueblo house.

Dying without a will can cause time-consuming and expensive legal procedures for your survivors, so if you really want to care for them and if you know how you want your estate distributed, you must make a Spanish will. It's easy and you will feel more secure.

ARE YOU BOUND BY SPANISH LAW?

This Spanish law of obligatory heirs in theory applies to foreigners with property in Spain, restricting the disposal of this property just as it restricts such disposal for Spaniards. This is because most nations apply the law of the place where the property is located.

However, Article 9 of the Spanish Civil Code provides that, when a foreign property owner dies, even if he holds an official residence permit, the disposal of any assets he has in Spain will be governed by his own national law, not Spanish law.

If his own country's law permits free disposal of the estate, this frees him from the Spanish law of "compulsory heirs" explained above. English law and United States law provide free disposition of assets. German law and Scottish law require that some portion of the estate go to surviving children. You must check your own national law here. (This article does not free the foreigner from Spanish inheritance taxes, however. See next section)

This freedom applies only when the foreigner has an existing foreign will or Spanish will. If he dies intestate, without having made a will, Spanish law will be applied to his assets in Spain and they will be divided equally among his children.

This is a powerful argument for making a Spanish will disposing of your assets in Spain according to your wishes.

For citizens of the United Kingdom, the first complication arises here. A number of countries, including Great Britain, have laws stating that the disposition of real property such as land, houses and apartments will be governed by the law of the country where such property is located. English law — which applies to Wales and Northern Ireland in this case, but not to Scotland — also states that other assets, such as investments, will be governed by the law of the country where the deceased is legally domiciled at the time of his death.

So Spanish law says that English law will apply, and English law sends the ball right back, saying that SPANISH law will apply, because that is where the property is located. An Englishman in theory is subject to the Spanish law, which may mean he can freely dispose of only one-third of his assets in Spain.

A number of other countries have laws similar to the English law. Investigate in your home country to find out what law applies to the disposition of real estate, the law of your home country or the law of the country where the immovable asset is located.

MOST FOREIGNERS HAVE FREE DISPOSITION

But what happens in practice?

In practice, any foreigner can make a Spanish will bequeathing his Spanish property to any person of his choice as long as his own national law is ruled by the principle of free disposition of property by testament. The Spanish registrar of wills accepts this. When the time comes, the will is executed and the inheritor takes possession of his new property. Spanish lawyers routinely make such wills.

This means that, even if you are British, you can make a Spanish will leaving your Spanish property to whomever you choose.

The law also says that any foreigner officially resident in Spain is subject to Spanish inheritance law on his world-wide estate.

In practice the authorities simply do not ask whether the testator is an official resident or not. They accept as valid the Spanish will disposing of only the Spanish property. The only requirement enforced by Spain is the payment of Spanish inheritance tax on property or assets located in Spain.

So most foreigners will find no problem in making a separate Spanish will to dispose of their immovable property in Spain, even though the law seems to say otherwise, whether they are residents or non-residents.

LEGITIMATE INHERITORS CAN CONTEST SPANISH WILL

One note of warning: All of the above relating to the foreigner's making a will that permits him to leave his Spanish property to anyone he chooses, thus avoiding Spanish inheritance law which requires him to leave at least two-thirds of his estate to his children, works perfectly well in most cases. But, as we have said, it is not exactly in agreement with the law as written. It is more a matter of the Spanish authorities choosing not to enforce their own laws too strictly.

This means that, if you write your Spanish will leaving your lovely villa to your favourite daughter and cutting out your no-good son entirely, that son could get expert Spanish legal advice, contest the will on the grounds that the law stipulates that half of the inheritance is his, and win his case, thus getting title to half the villa.

So, if you foresee any possible challenge from one of Spain's legitimate inheritors, such as a child or a spouse, you should make other arrangements, such as transferring the title of the property to your chosen heir while you are still alive. You can always maintain the usufruct over the property, which gives you the right to use it as long as you are still living, although the title has formally passed to another person.

If you are quite certain that no possibility exists of successfully contesting it, then go ahead and make your Spanish will as you choose in the confidence that it will be executed as you have written it.

You also need to make a foreign will disposing of any assets you have in other countries. Be sure that any foreign will states clearly that it disposes only of your assets in that country and make sure to say in your Spanish will that it disposes only of your assets in Spain.

There have been unfortunate cases where a person has made one will in Spain stating that all assets are left to one inheritor and another will later made in Germany or Australia, saying the same thing, but leaving "everything" to a different person.

In one particular case, the testator intended to leave all her German assets to family members and her Spanish villa to the friend who had looked after her for years. She made a Spanish will leaving everything to her friend in Spain and then made a German will, dated after the Spanish will, also leaving "everything" to her German family members.

These inheritors later had the German will translated and legalised in Spain, and took possession of the Spanish property as well.

They were able to do this because the German will made no distinction of country and it was dated after the Spanish will, so it took precedence. So, the testator's wishes were not carried out and the faithful friend who had looked after the ill and dying person in Spain did not inherit the villa as she was supposed to.

This story is a good argument for taking legal advice when you make your Spanish will.

FOREIGN WILL IS VALID IN SPAIN

Legally, it is not absolutely necessary for you to make a Spanish will to dispose of your assets in Spain. A Briton who owns property in Spain can bequeath his Spanish apartment in the same British will he uses to dispose of his property in England, and his will can be probated in Spain. However, there are a number of steps which must take place in order to do this.

If you have lived in Spain for a long time it may be necessary for you to re-create a legal domicile in your home country for purposes of making a will. You may be able to do this by filing an official "letter of intent" with your lawyers. This letter states that, even though you hold a Spanish residence permit now, you really intend to return to your home country in the end. This should be sufficient for establishing a legal domicile in your home country and will allow its laws to apply.

Let us suppose that you are able to establish domicile in your home country and that its laws will apply. Your foreign will (which can be made at your Consulate in Spain as long as the proper formalities are observed) must go through the following process before it can dispose of your Spanish assets:

A certified copy of the grant of probate must be legalised by the Spanish Consul in the testator's home country, and a Spanish translation of this certified copy prepared. A Spanish lawyer must then be empowered to prepare a list of the assets in Spain, see that the Spanish inheritance taxes are paid, and handle the rest of the paperwork involved in distributing the assets.

Two lawyers registered in your home country, or a notary, or a Spanish Consul-General in your home country, must prepare a certificate of law, a *certificado de ley,* which affirms that the testator had the legal capacity to make a will; that the will is valid; that the Spanish law of obligatory heirs and the dispositions relating to property of spouses do not exist in the law of your country; that the will has been duly proved, and that the trustees named have the correct legal powers to administer the estate.

Finally, your will is declared effective to dispose of your assets in Spain, and your Spanish lawyer can carry this out.

It's a complicated, time-consuming and expensive process, and it is clearly better to make a Spanish will disposing of your assets in Spain.

MAKING A SPANISH WILL

You go to see a Spanish lawyer and explain your wishes to him. In the case of the death of one spouse, for example, you may wish to leave all possible assets directly to the other spouse, without any inheritance to the children. As a foreigner, you should be able to do this.

Even if surviving children inherit their legal portion, it is not usually necessary for the house to be sold and the proceeds divided, for example. The surviving spouse continues to live in the house and administer it for the good of the children still at home. If the house is later sold, the children can then get their legal share of the price.

The lawyer will advise you as to how the will should read in order to carry out your intentions. People sometimes say that they want their Spanish flat sold and the proceeds divided among the children, for example. Your lawyer will tell you that you cannot do this. You must leave the flat to the children in equal parts. They can then sell it and divide the proceeds, but you cannot order its sale in your will. There may be other provisions on which your lawyer can advise.

The will is made out in two columns, one in Spanish and one in English, or in whatever language the testator prefers. The will is then checked by the *notario* and signed in his presence and that of three witnesses. This is called a *testamento abierto*, an open will, which is the usual form. The notary keeps the original in his files, gives you an authorised copy and sends a notification to the central registry in Madrid, called the *Registro Central de Ultima Voluntad*.

The certification numbers of all Spanish wills are kept on file here to ensure that a legal copy can always be found. If the will is lost or if you do not know whether the deceased person has made a Spanish will or not, you can apply to the central registry to find out if a Spanish will exists under that name. If it does exist, the registry will give you the number and the name of the notary who made it in the first place. You can get a copy of the will from the notary. Having a Spanish will certainly speeds up the legal processes of inheritance.

The notary will charge around   60 for the will and the lawyer's fee could be about the same, a total of   120, although this could go much higher if the will is complicated or involves large sums of money.

Remember that husband and wife must each make separate wills, as they each own property separately.

INHERITANCE TAX

You can also find out almost exactly how much inheritance tax your Spanish estate will attract. Your lawyer will consult the table of rates and then you will know what to expect.

All too often, the existence of Spanish inheritance tax seems to come as a complete surprise to foreign property owners. This tax is charged even when the inheritance is between spouses, with only a minimum exemption, as explained in the next section.

SECRET WILLS

Should you wish to keep secret the provisions of your will, you can also execute a *testamento cerrado,* a closed will. It is, of course, important to have a Spanish lawyer adivse you to make sure your wishes square with Spanish law. Otherwise, you might find your desires cannot lawfully be carried out. You take this closed will, in an envelope, to the *notario,* who seals the envelope and signs it along with the witnesses. He then files it, just as with the open will.

Other types of wills are also valid.

You can make a holographic will, in your own handwriting, but this later has to be authenticated as genuine before a judge, which means more time, trouble and expense. You can even make a verbal will, in the presence of five witnesses. Each of the five witnesses then has to testify to the *notario* that these are truly the wishes of the deceased. The *notario* then prepares a written will and certifies it.

INHERITANCE TAX IN SPAIN

Spain's *Ley de Sucesiones* provides no large exemption from inheritance tax when property is passed to a spouse or to family members, so many foreign property owners are dismayed to discover that some tax will be due.

Exemption Only   16,000: The present law provides a total exemption from taxes only for legacies under   16,000. To be exact, the exemption is   15,956.87. This long number results from the addition of yearly inflation to an original round number, plus the conversion from pesetas into euros. We shall call it simply   16,000.

The   16,000 exemption seems rather small, but it applies to each inheritor, not to the total estate. So, if you have a property worth   120,000, your half equals an estate valued at   60,000, and you leave it equally divided among your spouse and three children, each will receive an inheritance worth   15,000, and the bequest will attract no tax at all.

In addition, an inheritor under the age of 21 can have an exemption of up to   48,000. For each year younger than 21, he deducts   4,000 more, until he arrives at the maximum at the age of 13.

This exemption applies to bequests between parents, children, spouses and brothers and sisters. For uncles, cousins and nephews, the exemption is cut by half to   8,000. For more distant relatives, or those not related at all, there is no exemption.

Residents May Get 95 per cent Free Up to 120,000 euros

Official residents of Spain leaving their principal residence to wife or children, who are also official residents, may be eligible for a 95 per cent reduction in their tax base. This reduction rises to 99.9 per cent in Andalusia.

Three Conditions: There are three conditions for this reduction. They are:

You must have held an official residence permit for at least three years.

The home you transmit must be your principal residence and you must have lived in it for at least three years.

The inheritor must undertake not to sell the property for 10 years. If they do, they are subject to tax.

This reduction applies up to a maximum of   120,000.

That is, if your inheritance is a property worth   120,000, you can reduce this total by 95 per cent, taking off   114,000. So you pay tax on only   6,000, meaning no tax at all.

But if your family home in Spain has a market value of   360,000, then half of that is   180,000. Your reduction stops at the maximum of   120,000, meaning you must pay Spanish inheritance tax on   60,000, which comes to just over   6,000 in tax.

This reduction is also available for a principal dwelling left to a brother or sister over 65 years of age who has been living with the testator for the previous two years.

The reduction does not apply to any other property, such as a car or a yacht or shares in companies, only to the home itself.

The inheritor, in turn, must keep the property for at least 10 years. If she attempts to sell it, she will have to pay any tax due on the original inheritance.

This measure forms part of a package of laws designed to help small family businesses rather than retired foreigners. Many small businesses in Spain have failed on the death of the founder because his inheritors were unable to deal with the inheritance tax on the property, such as a shop or a small factory. Now the children can freely inherit, as long as they continue to operate the business for 10 years.

Retired foreign couples can also benefit, as described above, because the family home is included in the law. When one half of the couple dies, his or her share of the house or flat will be just about tax free to the surviving partner.

Non-residents cannot take advantage of this reduction.

ANDALUSIANS GET EXTRA TAX BREAK

In 2004 Andalusian tax authorities eliminated inheritance tax for family inheritors who are official residents of Andalusia and who receive less than   125,000. There are five conditions.

1. The testator must have been an official resident of Andalusia.
2. The inheritor, also a resident, must be a direct family member.
3. The total amount of the estate may not exceed   500,000.
4. The already-existing registered assets of each inheritor may not exceed   402,678.
5. Each individual inheritor may not inherit more than   125,000.

This exemption can be applied even to non-resident family inheritors if the testator has been a resident of Andalusia for the previous five years and dies as a resident in Andalusia.

Furthermore, this exemption is applied in addition to the reduction on the value of the family home. If you are all residents and do not intend to sell the home, you can leave a home worth 120,000 euros plus another 125,000 euros in other assets to a child free of inheritance tax.

The bad news is that, once the total amount of the estate exceeds 500,000, or each inheritor's share exceeds 125,000, the entire exemption disappears, and normal inheritance tax must be paid on he full amount.

Unmarried couples and same-sex couples who are registered with the Andalusian registry of de facto couples can also take advantage of this reduction.

HOW DOES SPAIN SET TAX VALUES?

Spain has a system for evaluating assets for purposes of inheritance tax. These are:

REAL ESTATE — Property is valued either at market price, or at the *valor catastral*, the rated value, or at the value set by the Tax Agency for purposes of wealth tax, whichever is greater. So, in almost all cases, you will find that the declared sales price on your title deed, or today's market value, is the value officially required. That is, if you bought your flat 20 years ago for 60,000, and it is worth 150,000 on the market today, Spain's tax agency values it at 150,000 for purposes of calculating inheritance tax.

But wait a minute. Market value or "real value" can vary up or down, depending on economic conditions. So, the Tax Agency generally accepts a lower figure, based on your *valor catastral*, the tax value discussed in Chapter Three. Now it gets complicated. This figure varies by Regions, even by municipalities. For example, on the Costa del Sol, authorities accept two times the rateable value in Mijas as a minimum declaration. Next door, in Benalmádena, the minimum figure is 1.6 times the *valor catastral*. You or your lawyer must ask what is the minimum acceptable value to declare in your area.

When you make your inheritance tax declaration, if you declare the flat as worth only 120,000, you might get away with it, or you might get a notice from Hacienda that they have valued it at 150,000 and you must pay tax on 30,000 more.

Remember that Hacienda has its own office of valuation and is perfectly aware of the market price of real estate. They will not fine you, but they will charge you the extra tax. They do this frequently.

If you disagree with their valuation, you can request an independent survey, a *tasación*.

PERSONAL EFFECTS — The furniture, clothing, personal

possessions and so on of the deceased are called the *ajuar*. For inheritance tax purposes they are routinely valued at 3 per cent of the price of the property. If valuable works of art or antique furniture pieces are included, they may be valued separately. In general, add 3 per cent of the property value to your estate.

AUTOMOBILES – Most property owners have automobiles, and these are included separately in the estate. Spain's Tax Agency publishes tables each year for the value of used cars. Other items, such as yachts or airplanes, will be valued separately.

STOCKS AND SHARES – Stocks and shares in companies or mutual funds or other investments are valued at their price on the day of the person's death.

LIFE INSURANCE – If received by children, the total amount is added to the estate, after a reduction of 9,000. If received by surviving spouse, half of the amount is added to the estate, and the other half is taxed as a capital gain in the spouse's yearly income tax. Spouse also has reduction of 9,000.

BANK ACCOUNTS – The balance on the day of death is added to the estate.

SOME SPANISH REGIONS HAVE DIFFERENT SCALES

NOTE that some of Spain's Autonomous Regions have different tax scales for inheritance. Madrid, Catalonia and the Valencian Community, using their independence from the central State Government, have prepared their own inheritance tax scales.

NOTE also that Madrid, both a city and a province, has added to its inheritance laws that an unmarried couple who are registered in the registry of common-law couples, can take advantage of the lower tax rates applied to married couples. This is not true in most other regions, except for Andalusia.

SPANISH INHERITANCE TAX RATES YEAR 2005

Euros – rounding centimos

Tax Base	Tax	Marginal Percentage
0.00	0.00	7.65
7,993	611	8.50
15,980	1,290	9.35
23,968	2,037	10.20
31,955	2,852	11. 05
39,943	3,735	11. 90
47,930	4,685	12.75
55,918	5,703	13.60
63,905	6,790	14.45
71,893	7,944	15.30
79,880	9,166	16.15
119,757	15,606	18.70
159,634	23,063	21. 25
239,389	40,011	25.50
398,777	80,655	29.75
797,555	199,291	34.00

How to Use the Tax Table: A Sample Calculation

You can calculate your own inheritance tax by using the tables shown here.

1. **Figure Total Value:** Figure your total value by referring to the section above on valuations.

2. **Reductions:** You can then subtract from this amount any debts owed by the deceased. This would include a mortgage still unpaid on the property, for example. You can also deduct the expenses of the last illness and the funeral and burial.

3. **Refusal of Inheritance:** In cases where the debts of an estate are greater than the assets, which could happen when a small business constitutes the estate, for example, the inheritors can refuse to accept the inheritance, thus being free of their parent's debts.

4. **Calculation:** After you have made any deductions allowed you for the inheritance tax, such as your basic exemption of   15,956.87, if the estate is passing to close family, let's suppose that your final taxable inheritance is about   42,000.

Look at the table to find the nearest figure below that amount. In this case it is   39,943. The tax due on that amount is   3,735.

Now you need to consult the marginal percentage list, for the rate charged on the difference between the steps.

In your case you find that you must pay 11.90 per cent of the difference between   39,943 and your inheritance of   42,000.

The difference is   2,057. Multiply this by 11.90 percent and this gives you another   244.78. Add the two together and you have a total tax of   3,980, a little less than 10 per cent of your base.

These numbers were originally nice round numbers like five million in pesetas, but they have been increased according to inflation since the law was originally passed, and even more decimals arose when they were converted directly and exactly into euros.

RICH PAY MORE

From the table, it looks as if 34 per cent is the absolute top rate of Spanish inheritance tax. This is true when the estate is passed in direct line of descent or between spouses. But it can be much higher when bequests are made to more distant relatives or to non-relatives. And it can be even higher when the inheritor is already wealthy. Remember that the sliding scale of Spanish inheritance tax is designed to favour the poor and soak the rich.

This scale provides multiplying coefficients for the degree of relationship and also for the amount of existing wealth of the inheritor. To get the amount of tax due from those who are more distant relatives or non-related and those who already have sizeable fortunes, you must multiply the basic tax rates above by the coefficients given in the table below.

Existing Assets	Spouses Children	Cousins Uncles	Non-Relatives
0 to 402,678	1.0000	1.5882	2.0000
402,678 to 2,007,380	1.0500	1.6676	2.1000
2,007,388 to 4,020,770	1.1000	1.7471	2.2000
More than 4,020,770	1.2000	1.9059	2.4000

So, if you are fortunate enough to possess assets worth more than four million euros, and you inherit more than 797,555 from someone who is not related to you, the Spanish tax ministry will multiply the 34 per cent by the 2.4 coefficient and will demand a tax from you of 81.6 per cent.

This system penalises inheritance to non-relations because it is designed to protect the family structure as well as the poor. It has caused problems for same-sex couples and for couples who may have lived together for many years in a stable relationship but are not married.

The high rate of inheritance tax and low exemptions in Spain cause many to seek ways round paying it, some of which are legal, some not.

CAN YOU AVOID SPANISH TAX?

Power of Attorney Not Valid:
A note of warning: Many Britons have been misled by the wording in English of an "Enduring Power of Attorney".

Such a power of attorney does not mean that the power endures beyond the death of the person who grants it. A power of attorney dies with its maker, in Spain and in the UK. The "enduring" simply means that it has no other fixed date of expiry.

People sometimes think that such a power of attorney will allow them to dispose of property, such as a villa in Spain, after the death of the owner, thus avoiding the formalities of a will and inheritance tax.

This is not so. The power of attorney legally expires when the maker of it dies. Some people have used the trick of failing to inform the authorities of the death and then using the power of attorney to sell a property. If swiftly done, the authorities are not likely to catch you, but it is against the law. Further, if someone had reason to protest such a sale, they could have it annulled as a fraudulent act.

Nevertheless, such a power of attorney can be very useful for persons who have aged parents in Spain because it allows the child to manage the property and finances of the granter of the power. It is easy to obtain and is used in Spain for the same reasons as in the UK or other country.

A "General Power of Attorney" a *poder general,* is frequently used in Spain. The power comes in a standard form, which lists all of the actions that can be carried out by the holder. These include buying and selling property, handling bank accounts, spending and receiving money, taking out a mortgage or other loan, and just about anything that the person himself can do with his assets.

The form contains a clause declaring that all of these actions shall be taken for the benefit of the granter of the power. This means that, if you decide to take the money and run, the granter has a case against you for defrauding him, if he can find you.

There are also other forms of power of attorney, limited to carrying out certain specific actions in the name of the granter, such as signing a contract for the sale of a specified property at a given price, during a given time period, after which the power lapses.

But the general power is the one most used, simply because situations change and unforeseen complexities arise in any transaction. This can mean that the holder of the power is unable to act because the power does not mention the specific circumstance which has arisen, such as signing at the bank to obtain the money transfer from abroad.

The wide powers of the general power of attorney avoid these problems. In an international property market, we often find that a seller or a buyer cannot be physically present at the moment of signing a purchase deed at the Spanish Notary, so he gives his lawyer or some other trusted person a general power of attorney to sign for him.

Once the deed is accomplished, the granter then revokes the power of attorney, again at the Notary, and all goes on as before.

The only possible hitch is whether your aged parent wishes to grant you all of these powers. In the usual circumstances, however, the aged parent is only too glad to have all these matters taken off his hands.

In that case, he need only make an appointment with the nearest Spanish Notary. Although it is always a good idea to consult a lawyer before taking any important legal step, it is not necessary.

The Notary has the power of attorney forms, probably in his computer, which will print copies for you while the Notary himself retains the original power of attorney. A reminder: you need copies authorised by the Notary in order to use the power of attorney at a bank or in a property sale. The simple copies you can also obtain are for information only.

The only documents necessary are the national identity document or the passport of the maker of the power. He will need the name and identity document or passport details of the holder.

The entire operation should not cost much more than 60. Yes, it all seems too simple and too cheap for such a wide-ranging document, but there you are.

The recipient of the power of attorney does not need to appear at the Notary. The document requires his signature, but he can do this at his own convenience. So the maker of the power can simply post it to the recipient.

Family Trust: Among the perfectly legal possibilities is the formation of a family corporation or trust, in which the family's wealth passes into the hands of the company, with each family member becoming a director of the company. So when one member of the family dies, it involves only a reorganisation of the board of directors and a transfer of some of the company shares, attracting very little tax.

Off-shore Company: For non-Spaniards, the constitution of a Gibraltar-based company or other offshore operation in order to own real property in Spain has been another way to avoid Spanish inheritance taxes. In this case, when the founder of the company dies he leaves his shares in the company to whomever he chooses, in a will made outside of Spain. But as far as Spain is concerned, the same company continues to own the property and no transfer has taken place, hence there is no tax. See chapter on Taxes for more information but be warned that Spain has placed a special tax on properties owned by companies registered in off-shore tax havens. You will need expert legal advice on your individual circumstances and the possible disadvantages of this offshore ownership before you decide.

Four-Year Limit: Another trick takes advantage of the fact that the statute of limitations on inheritance tax, and all other taxes, runs out after four years. That is, the State cannot collect the tax once four years have elapsed. So the scheme is to "lose" the deceased's will for four years, not declaring the property for inheritance. At the end of four years, the inheritor "discovers" the will and takes possession of the property, free of any inheritance tax. Where the estate is large and the tax is high, this plan can be worth it.

Be warned, however, that Spanish law requires that an inheritance be declared within six months of the death, and if you are found out, you can be subject to a surcharge of 25 per cent on the tax due, or even higher penalties if the Spanish authorities rule that deliberate fraud is involved. Also be warned that the six-month period is included in the statute of limitations, so you really have to wait four years and six months for *prescripción*, the Spanish term for statute of limitations.

Gift: You can also make a gift of the property to your inheritors while you are still living, perhaps reserving the right to inhabit the flat as long as you live, but remember that the Spanish gift tax is exactly the same as the inheritance tax. The law in fact is called the Law on Inheritance and Gifts.

"Sell" Property Now: Or you might "sell" your property to your heir, again reserving the *usufructo* or lifetime right to inhabit it yourself. At property transfer costs of around 10 per cent, this could save your inheritor a sizeable sum when the valuation is more than 50,000 and the inheritor is a non-relative.

You have to go on living for at least five years after you carry out this operation, however, or the State will assume that you did it only to avoid tax and will charge you the full amount.

This particular method has many attractions for same-sex couples where one party owns the property and wishes to leave it to the other, without suffering the very high rate of taxation applied to non-relatives.

Buy in Name of Inheritor
Planning ahead can save you money. If you are sure that you want your children to inherit your Spanish property and you are already advanced in years, you can make your original purchase in the name of the child or other inheritor. When you buy, at the same time you reserve to yourself that lifetime right to use, the *usufructo*. When you die, your inheritors simply take possession of their property.

Each case needs individual study so it makes sense to consult a Spanish lawyer when making your will.

GLOSSARY

Ajuar – The contents of a home, furnishings and equipment

Certificado de Ley – Certificate of Law, usually certifying that the law of another country is applicable.

Exención – Exemption

Herederos Forzosos – Compulsory heirs

Pareja de Hecho – Unmarried couple living together as man and wife

Poder – Power of Attorney

Prescripción – Time limit on legal action, statute of limitations

Registro Central de Ultima Voluntad – Central Registry of Wills

Tasación – valuation, of property or other asset

Testamento – Will, testament

Testamento Cerrado – Secret, closed will

Ultima Voluntad – Last will and testament

Usufructo – Usufruct, right to enjoy

Valor Catastral – Officially rated value of property

7.   YOUR COMMUNITY OF PROPERTY OWNERS

When you buy a property in Spain – as more than one million foreigners already have done – you automatically become a member of a community of property owners, whether you like it or not. Whether the property is your retirement home or a holiday flat, whether it is an apartment, a townhouse or a detached villa on an urbanisation, you will find your own interests affected by the community and the decisions of your neighbours. You will pay your community fees every year, and you will meet with your neighbours at the Annual General Meeting to argue about whether to paint the outside of the building or whether to fire the gardener.

If your building or urbanisation is new, you may even take part in the original organisation of the community, with all its problems of drafting the statutes, electing a president, fixing the amount of community fees, planning the budget and defining the relation of the property promoter and his still unsold properties to the rest of the community.

Only those who buy an individual house in a town street or a farmhouse on a large tract of rural land will not have to deal with belonging to a Spanish *Comunidad de Propietarios*. A well-run community can add thouands of euros of value to an otherwise unremarkable house,

131

and a poorly run community can cut thousands off the value of even a very nice apartment.

Before you buy any Spanish property, find out as much as you can about the operations of the community. See the list of questions to ask in the Capsule Guide that follows.

Over the years problems arising from community life have produced hundreds of letters to my magazine columns and many, many telephone calls to my radio programmes. People want to know if the Annual General Meeting can be held in English, how to fire an administrator who is not properly serving the interests of all the owners, how to form a legal community on an unregistered urbanisation, how to collect community fees from non-payers, and dozens of other matters.

This brief guide hopes to answer some of these questions. For a more complete treatment of communities, see *You and the Law in Spain,* which contains a complete translation of the Law of Horizontal Property into English, along with explanatory comments

WHAT IS A COMMUNITY?

THE COMMUNITY OF PROPERTY OWNERS - *comunidad de propietarios* - is the Spanish system for regulating the joint ownership of common property. In an apartment building this means the entranceway, the staircases, the lift, the roof space, the grounds and any other shared spaces used by all the owners. On an urbanisation it will include the roads, gardens, communal pools, lighting system, drains and other services.

This type of ownership is often called "condominium" in English, for co-ownership. The community sets out the manner in which all the co-owners manage their joint affairs for the best administration of the shared property. The co-owners must decide how much money they want to pay for the maintenance and management of their building and grounds, and exactly how this money will be spent.

The law which regulates this system is called the Law of Horizontal Property - *la Ley de Propiedad Horizontal.* This law, originally passed in 1960 and amended in 1999, was actually more vertical than horizontal in its original version because it applied mainly to apartment buildings, although it also covered townhouse developments of attached units. Provisions of the 1999 changes have made it much easier for urbanisations of detached villas to use the protection of the Horizontal Law.

Nevertheless, many urbanisations are regulated by other laws included in several sections of the Land Law, the *Ley del Suelo*. These communities may be of several sorts, but the most effective are called *Entidad Urbanística Colaboradora de Gestión y Conservación*. This mouthful translates as "collaborating urbanistic entity of management and maintenance," and is often shortened to EUC. Estates of detached villas sometimes require a different body of law because they present different problems. The roads, drains and lighting installations of the urbanisation may serve the public as well as the residents, thus having a quasi-public aspect which requires collaboration between the urbanisation owners and the Town Hall authorities. This interaction between the town and the estate demands extra regulation not needed in the case of apartment buildings.

But in both cases the idea of the law is the same: to provide a framework in which the community becomes a legal force. It can go to court, enforce the payment of community fees, and make contracts. It can also be sued itself. Many problems have arisen in communities of detached villas because they were not originally formed according to the correct laws.

BEFORE YOU BUY

When you buy property in Spain, you become a member of the community of property owners. You should know five things about this community before you sign any purchase contract.

Ask these five questions:

1. How much will I have to pay each year in community charges?

Whether you buy an apartment, a townhouse or a detached villa, the property will have a participation share assigned to it, the *cuota*, which determines the amount of the yearly fees for community expenses. This can vary from as little as 50 a month in a modest apartment building up to 400 a month and even more on a luxurious urbanisation with many services to maintain.

These fees can be expected to rise with the general cost of living. The community members may have unexpected expenses, such as repairing the lift or the roof, or they may vote improvements which will add to the costs.

Keep in mind that community fees only cover the operating and maintenance of the building or estate. In addition, you will have to pay your individual annual real estate taxes and your water and electricity bills.

Ask your seller for his last paid-up community fee receipt. He is obligated by law to justify this or to declare the amount of the debt. If this is not possible, you can find out your property's share and any debts by asking the promoter of the building or the president of the community.

2. Are the community fees paid up to date?

The Horizontal Law requires the President of the Community to produce a certificate stating that the property's fees are paid up, or listing the amount of the debt owed. The seller of the property should arrange for this. In any case, the buyer can be held liable only for the Community fees of this year and last year.

3. Can I see the community statutes?

Of course you can, and you can learn many things from them about life in your new property. Remember that the regulations of the statutes will be binding on you as a member of the community. If they prohibit dogs, you will not be able to keep Rover, for example.

Many sales contracts contain a clause in which the buyer states that he accepts the statutes of the community, understands them and agrees to abide by them. Even when there is not such a reference, the buyer is legally bound when he becomes the owner of the property. He cannot refuse to join a community which legally exists. (Some urbanisations do not, in fact, have a legal community).

Ask your seller, the president of the community, or the real estate promoter of a new building for a copy of the Statutes. If they are not available, it may mean problems ahead for you, which brings us to the next question.

4. Does the community legally exist?

Sometimes a community of property owners does not have a proper legal existence, even when required by law. This can occur in a new building or urbanisation when sales are not yet completed and the community has not yet been constituted and its statutes registered with the Property Registry, in the case of apartment buildings, or the Registry of Conservation Entities, in the case of an urbanisation. Yes, a properly constituted community is registered in the Property Registry. After all, it owns property, such as the garden spaces or the roads.

This legal vacuum can also occur when an established urbanisation either is illegal and unregistered or when the owners have formed their association under laws not properly designed for communities of property owners. Unless these associations of owners are registered and the new buyers agree in their contracts to abide by the statutes, their rules may not be legally enforceable. Don't get too excited about disobeying the rules, by not paying the charges, for example, because Spanish courts have often ruled that such associations have a *de facto* existence, and a right to collect the fees for the common good.

Ask to see the legal registration of the community in one of the registries listed above.

If the community does not yet exist or is not properly registered, you will sooner or later have problems to sort out, either in the formation of the community or in making it a legal body. In either case, lawyers will be involved and there will be fees to pay.

5. Is the community in debt?

If the community has had to borrow money in order to pay for unexpected repairs on the building, you will assume your share of this debt when you become a member. Inform yourself in advance.

See the Minutes Book: You can find out this and many other things by looking at the official minutes of the last Annual General Meeting of the community, along with the accounts.

Your seller should have a copy of the minutes and the accounts. If he has not, you can obtain them from the president of the community or from the promoter of the real estate where you are purchasing.

A reading of the minutes will give you an idea of the sort of problems and expenses that arise in this particular community. It will contain a record of the voting as well, so that you can see if one individual has voted the proxies of many others, as often happens in communities where many of the owners are absent from their properties much of the time.

If the minutes show that the principal business of the last meeting was how to deal with the persistent water problems or with the backlog of unpaid fees, you will know you have trouble ahead.

These official minutes will be in Spanish, but it is well worth your time to have at least a rough translation made. The administrator or president of the community is obliged by law to keep these records at the disposal of the members.

YOUR RIGHTS AND OBLIGATIONS

As a member of the community of property owners, you have the right to attend the Annual General Meeting, and any other meetings of the community, along with the right to be properly informed in advance of the dates and the order of business of any meeting called. If you are not correctly informed, you can protest and even have the results of the meeting annulled by a court.

At the meeting you have the right to voice your opinion, the right to vote, and to present motions for the vote of the other members.

You have the right to be elected and to hold office in the community. You may be the president, the vice-president or the secretary. You may be charged with administrating the affairs of the community.

You have the right to see all of the documentation and records of the community. The administrator or other officers are legally bound to keep these records and accounts at the disposal of the members. If they refuse to show them to you, you can obtain a court order to see the documents.

You have the right to hold and to vote proxies issued by other members who are absent from the meeting. This is common practice in communities where the foreign owners are absent much of the time. Most communities in fact have a standard Proxy Form on which an absent member can delegate his vote to another member. If you win the confidence of many members and obtain enough proxy votes, you can run the community to suit yourself.

If you feel that a decision voted by the majority of the community is illegal or contrary to the statutes, you, acting alone, can ask the local court to rule on the matter. If you feel that the decision is legal, but seriously prejudicial to your own interests, and you can unite 25 per cent of the owners and shares, you can petition the court to have the decision annulled, or you can oblige the president to call an Extraordinary General Meeting. You will need skilled legal counsel for either of these actions.

You are obligated to pay the *cuotas* - community fees which have been properly voted by the members at the Annual General Meeting. If you do not pay, the community can claim the debt in court and even have your property sold at auction.

You are obligated to abide by the statutes of the community. If these statutes require all owners to paint their properties white and forbid owners to keep dogs, then you must paint your property white and you may not keep a dog. If you violate the statutes, the community members can vote to ask the court to issue an injunction which will forbid you from entering your property for a period of up to two years. This seldom occurs but the threat is there and it has been carried out in a few isolated cases.

Both the Law of Horizontal Property and the statutes of most communities make provision for such obligations as maintaining your property in good condition so that it does not cause damage to the other owners, and permitting workmen to enter your property when it is necessary for repairs on the building.

THE PRESIDENT

The only community officer required by law is the president. He must be elected from among the members of the community, and he can carry out all the administrative work if no other officers are elected or appointed.

The president acts as the legal representative of the community in action. He signs contracts and cheques and can bring lawsuits in the name of the community when he is authorised by the vote of the general meeting. He himself can be sued by the community if the members feel his actions have prejudiced their interests. If the community is sued, perhaps by someone who fell through a badly maintained balustrade, the president, acting through a lawyer, will be their representative in court. The President gives orders to the Administrator.

The president will prepare the notices of general meetings, along with the order of business. He will see that the notices are sent out well in advance. He will oversee the preparation of the accounts of expenditures and income and he will prepare the budget for the coming year. He makes sure that the minutes of the meeting are carefully kept and notarised. He presides over the meeting and informs the absent members in writing of the decisions taken. If they do not register any protest within 30 days, their agreement to the decisions is assumed.

The president, when acting as the sole officer of the community, will oversee the management of the common elements of the property, will hear the complaints of the community members, and has full responsibility for the operation of the community, subject only to the approval of the annual general meeting.

The president is so important that the law says the community must never be without one. The usual term of office is one year, although the statutes may specify other time periods, but if the community does not act to elect a new president when the time is up, the old one continues in office until a new president is elected.

Many small communities where the president is the only officer find difficulty in persuading one of the members to take on this time-consuming responsibility. In many buildings, the flat owners take it in turn each year to be the president.

Since passage of the 1999 law, the president can even be paid for his services.

THE ADMINISTRATOR

Because many details demand the attention of the person who runs a community, most larger communities choose to name a professional Administrator for this job. The administrator is contracted to manage the services of the community and is paid a regular fee for this service.

Many communities choose to employ a licenced *Administrador de Fincas,* a professional property administrator, or a licenced tax consultant or accountant, but the community administrator need not hold any official title. In many smaller communities, the President is also the Administrator.

People sometimes think that the professional administrator is an elected officer of the community. This is not so. He is a hired professional, usually contracted for a period of one year. The community may vote to renew his contract, vary his payment, or name a new administrator at the annual general meeting. The president may terminate the services of the administrator at any time if he feels that the administrator is not carrying out the duties specified in his contract. This decision must be submitted to the general meeting for approval, but this can take place after the action.

Relations between communities and their professional administrators have caused many problems. The administrator's contract must be very carefully drafted to make sure that both parties know their rights and duties.

The administrator's duties are the normal ones of seeing to the proper management of the common elements of the community. Unless otherwise specified in the Statutes of a particular community, the Horizontal Law says that the administrator shall prepare the budget and present it to the meeting; maintain the building; inform the owners of his activities and carry out any other function conferred by the general meeting.

Many administrators carry out the work of the community effectively and rapidly, doing their best to keep all of the owners satisfied and well informed. They charge a reasonable fee for their services and they present the community members with clear accounts each year at the general meeting. These administrators are treasures.

In other cases, members complain that the administrators do not carry out the work for which they are responsible, that they arrange community affairs to suit themselves rather than the members, and that their accounts are vague and confusing. These administrators should be replaced.

Replacing the administrator, like electing the president, is an important step and will require the majority vote of the community members. This brings us to the Annual General Meeting.

ANNUAL GENERAL MEETING

The Annual General Meeting is the maximum authority of the community of property owners. They are required by law to meet at least once each year to elect a president, discuss issues affecting the community, to examine and approve the accounts of expenditures of the previous year and to decide upon the budget - and the fees each member will pay - for the coming year.

The book of minutes, the *libro de actas*, which records details of the meeting and the voting, is an official legal document which can be used in Spanish court proceedings. It must be stamped as authentic by a notary or a judge. This book establishes the right of the community president in court to bring a lawsuit against a community member who has not paid his fees, the *cuotas*. It should record the names of members who voted in favour of a measure, either in person or by proxy, and the names of those who voted against each measure. This becomes important when a minority of community members wish to bring a legal protest against the decision of the majority, claiming that their interests have been seriously damaged, even though the majority vote was otherwise quite in order. In a court case, the dissenting minority must bring action against the majority. So the minutes book, as a legal document, establishes the names of those who voted on either side. The book is evidence in court, and decisions made by the community are serious matters.

Before you attend your first meeting, you should try to meet the president and the administrator of your community, as well as other members, to get an idea of the problems facing the members. If you already have a motion that you want passed by community vote, you can begin to assemble the proxy votes of members who support your position and who will be absent from the meeting. This proxy can be a simple written authorisation that enables you to cast the vote of the absentee.

You must be notified at least eight days in advance of the meeting's date, time and place. You should also receive a written agenda, the order of business to be transacted, though this is not strictly necessary. The members can bring up any new business they wish at the meeting. It need not be listed on the agenda.

At the meeting, you will register your attendance, and any proxies you will vote, with the secretary or keeper of the minutes book. The president will preside over the meeting. The first item will be the reading and vote to approve the minutes of the previous meeting. If the minutes do not meet with your approval, either because they are false or incomplete, you can vote against accepting them. Your protest will be registered in the book and can serve as evidence in court if you wish to make a claim.

The accounts of the previous year's income and expenditures will then be presented for the members' approval. You should have received your copy of these accounts before the meeting. Sometimes they are perfectly clear and other times they are quite incomprehensible. Ask the president, administrator or treasurer to explain any points not clear to you.

Then discussion will start on plans and expenses for the coming year. Many issues can arise. Perhaps one group wishes to paint the building or to install a swimming pool, but others protest that this will raise the fees too high.

Tempers can run high at community meetings. They sometimes degenerate into multilingual shouting matches when not properly managed. At one meeting a woman became enraged when she felt she was not getting her fair chance to speak and she threw an ashtray at the table of the presiding officers. A heavy ashtray.

Even in the best of circumstances, meetings tend to be longwinded, as different members insist on discussing minor details. One community I know voted unanimously to limit each member's speaking time to five minutes, and to limit each member to two speeches.

When it is time to vote, you will vote according to your *cuota*, or community share. This *cuota*, based on the size of your property, determines both your share of community fees and the weight of your vote. Usually, the majority of members is also the majority of the *cuotas*, but sometimes a few members with large properties can dominate the workings of a community. This can happen on an urbanisation where the developer still controls the votes of the unsold parcels of land and runs the community to suit himself.

The Horizontal Law establishes that a majority vote must be counted by both number of owners and amount of *cuotas*. If many owners with small shares vote one way and a few owners with large shares vote the other way, you have a disputed vote. Generally, Spanish courts decide in favour of the larger number of owners and not the larger amount of shares.

The votes of the members will be recorded in the minutes book and action will be taken accordingly. A new president will be elected by majority vote and the building will be painted or not, according to the majority decision. There is always the possibility of protest, remember, when a minority of members feel they have been pushed around by the majority.

If a decision requires a unanimous vote, such as a change in the statutes or a construction project which will alter the participation shares of the community members, this unanimity can be achieved by informing any absent members of the decision. If they do not respond negatively within one month the motion is considered as passed unanimously.

The Horizontal Law provides that the installation of ramps and other facilities for the handicapped requires only a three-fifths majority, even when such an alteration of the building would normally need a unanimous vote. This does not exactly give the handicapped a free rein, but it does improve their negotiating position. This means that one person in a building cannot block the installation of ramps.

Finally the meeting will be adjourned, with some members pleased and others not pleased at all. This is truly democracy in action, with all its advantages and disadvantages.

When people are unhappy with their community, they always refer to it as "they." The community is never "they." It is always "we".

WHAT TO DO IF:

You are unhappy with your community
The problem with a Community of Property Owners is that it functions as a democracy. The vote of the owners is the final authority. If you wish to change something, you must win a vote. This means that you yourself must engage in active politics. You must solicit the votes of other owners by explaining your case to them. It takes your time and effort but winning the vote is the only final solution.